key moments in

Hamlyn

Archit

the relationship between man, buildings and urba

ecture

rowth as seen in the metropolis through the ages

Graham Vickers

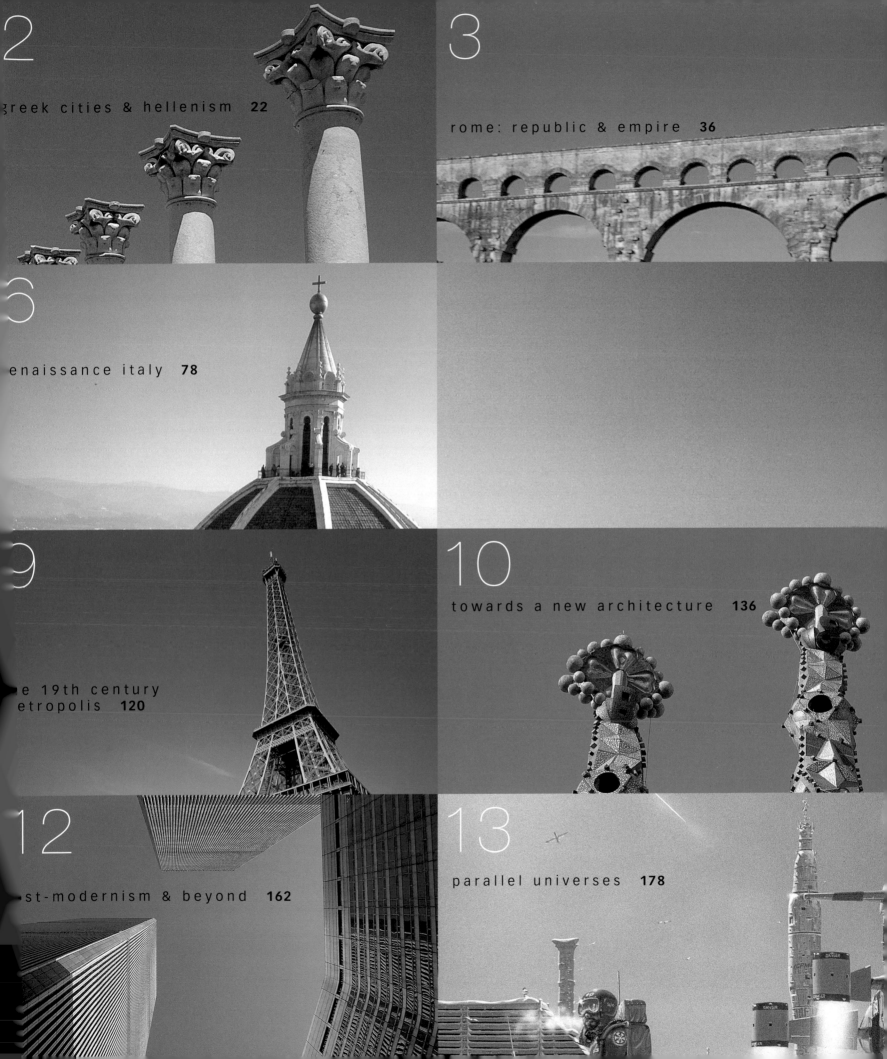

the origins of the city

1

the anatomy of the city

Most of us are so familiar with the city in some form or other, that it is difficult for us to look at it with fresh eyes. If we did – if for example we were to have arrived on earth from another planet at any time during the past three or four thousand years – the first thing we would have seen on our approach would have been the physical shapes of earth's cities.

Precisely what we would have seen would depend when we arrived. However certain physical facts hold true across time, even if the reasons behind them are not immediately apparent from the material evidence.

There are certain defining aspects of cities, visual clues to the nature of the beast. An extra-terrestrial visitor to earth might begin to grasp these more obvious physical aspects of the city simply by observing. No matter how visually stimulating the experience, it would leave far more interesting questions unasked and unanswered. Questions such as, What is the spirit of the city? What is it about human beings that makes the city apparently indivisible from life on earth?

Cities are not just buildings. They are a curiously potent compound of buildings and people. The way people create, use and interact with the fabric of their urban concentrations make for a single entity. It is that entity which this book seeks to explore by taking a bird's eye view of the City in Time and exploring how the medium of architecture has, over the centuries, given us what we want – or at least what we deserve.

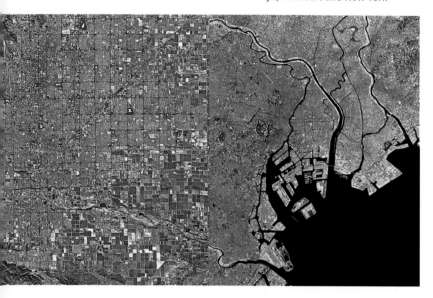

left to right Satellite images of the urban patterns of Phoenix Arizona, Tokyo, Frankfurt and New York

8

Cities tend to come in clusters

Those clusters form a kind of urban hierarchy. That is to say, every city has its satellite townships, just as every town has its outlying villages. The pattern seems to have existed everywhere across history, uniting even those cities with very different cultures and provenance.

Cities emerge from the countryside

Increasingly difficult to justify in the modern era, this precept remains true in essence. It was never truer than in the cities of antiquity when every feature of the surrounding landscape conditioned the shape and character of the urban form. Today the 'pre-fabricated' city – the city that could sit almost anywhere – is closer to feasibility than ever before, but history repeatedly reminds us that Urban Engineering often loses out to a more natural process of evolutionary development: consider, for example, all those now abandoned 19th century railway lines that were supposed to form the skeletons of new, thriving ribbon development towns, but somehow never did.

Cities always have their limits

No longer always physically pronounced, city limits always exist even if only in the statute book. Without city walls – even symbolic ones – a city is not a city.

Cities have comparatively dense concentrations of people

'Comparatively' because there are no absolute numbers involved in defining a city. What distinguishes a city is the contrast between the numbers of outlying areas and the concentration of numbers within.

Cities are places where a wide variety of work exists

This variety creates a social hierarchy. Cities have both rich people and poor people. Money and therefore power can be seen to be unequally distributed.

Cities always have written records

The social structures described here are to some extent conceptual, and the concepts on which they depend have to be recorded. Records need facilities for storage and, until recent times, this often demanded substantial premises located within the city itself.

Cities have monumental buildings

Whatever the dominating characteristic of the city in time – religious, secular or military – monuments will be built or adapted. Purely practical residential and commercial buildings are not enough to satisfy the City's sense of itself and the importance of its dominant culture. Yesterday's cathedral might become today's People's Palace, but monuments of some sort or another will emerge.

architecture and the city

Architecture affects everyone. More than any other kind of design, architecture touches us all, partly because of its scale and its public nature, and partly because it holds up a very revealing mirror to the kind of society in which we live. Architecture first of all reflects how we feel about ourselves and then, because it defines the spaces and institutions with which we live, it goes on to condition how we behave. The evidence can be seen everywhere that buildings are built. The built environment reflects civic priorities, government policies, our attitudes about our work, our leisure, our neighbours and ourselves.

At a very obvious level, cities with wide boulevards and open spaces reflect and encourage quite different patterns of social behaviour than do cities with small, tight street plans. They feel different and they are different. No one could confuse New York with Seville, Mexico City with Copenhagen. In fact the same basic human demands made of any city have been customised so specifically that we complain when chains of international hotels replicate themselves unvaryingly in every city: 'you could be anywhere' we say, revealing an implicit fondness for urban variety. In fact variety endures, for any number of reasons and motives, not all of them good. The pedestrian is an outcast in Los Angeles; the car driver is a slow-motion prisoner in Amsterdam. Any metropolis bristling with skyscrapers has a culture quite distinct from that of any low-rise, low-density city. Shopping for food in Paris, whose development has favoured a multiplicity of small, central speciality shops, is a totally different experience from shopping for food in London where one-stop-shop out of town supermarkets dominate.

A city whose architecture looks to the future reflects a very different set of social and cultural ambitions from one that is defined largely by its historical monuments. Cities with hot climates once built open arcades or narrow alleys for shade and ventilation; Victorian cities with more variable climates favoured elaborate glazed arcades for protection. Both live on in cities where shopping is now largely done elsewhere. Any city with no-go zones is an unwitting monument to the divisive society it houses. Singapore's relatively new underground railway system is a mass transit masterpiece; London's old underground railway system – the first in the world – is now scarcely adequate for modern city needs. Cities are all the same; cities are all different. All cities change at different rates.

New cities like Kuala Lumpur grow at an unprecedented rate. However, except in the relatively rare cases of wholesale destruction followed by widespread rebuilding, the fabric of existing cities is often relatively slow to reflect change. When such a city changes, it usually does so in a progressive, piecemeal way, with elements that are slow to change co-existing with more urgent architectural adventures.

For this reason, the social preferences and the aspirations of those who planned and built yesterday's cities often live on beyond their natural time in the fragmented urban inheritances of subsequent generations. In a modern age of instant communications, rapid reinvention, planned obsolescence and short expectations, this tendency has made 'appropriate' architecture a far more problematical concept for many people than it used to be. Views quickly become divided between those who wish to preserve and those who wish to demolish and rebuild – not to mention those who hold a whole series of subtler, less polarised opinions. Urban architecture, unlike so many other contemporary man-made artifacts and concepts, is no neat and consistent entity; rather it is a continuum of possibilities and therefore also an almost infinite source of potential disagreement. That said, the 'modern' architecture of any age has always provoked heated debate to some extent, and this eternal ability to raise passions may be taken as further evidence of city architecture's visceral relationship with mankind.

City architecture can move us to joy, excitement or despair, depending on the impulses, values, skills and politics that brought it about. It can unite or alienate. Human beings have created cathedrals magnificent enough to move the staunchest of non-believers, but they have also built ghettoes brutal enough to make the saints abandon hope. Good or bad, our architecture is the visible and tangible expression of our society's taste, culture, politics and preoccupations. City architecture, quite simply, is a continuing monument to what we are.

left The city's design is dictated by its function; in the case of modern Los Angeles, this is dominated by the need to accommodate and facilitate the automobile as primary transport

Basic Building Forms

Until the 20th century, there were only two basic building methods: frame and skin or blocks piled one on top of the other. Infinite varieties of block building were possible, using mud, stone and all kinds of brick. Frame and skin structures originally varied in accordance with the climate and local materials at hand, although the classic example remains that of the teepee, an elegantly minimal and highly stable structure of animal hide tightly wrapped around a conical skeleton of sticks. Both systems have endured for around 10,000 years and are still in use today, alongside the sudden variety of new techniques made possible only by technologies developed in the past 100 years.

Contemporary examples of block building exist in brick-built houses, walls and countless stone structures. The contemporary frame and skin buildings, in which coverings of various materials including glass and insulated panels hang from rigid infrastructures, are really only more sophisticated versions of the age-old principle.

below Las Ramblas, Barcelona, a pedestrian-friendly city thoroughfare where the motor car is not king

At the same time, architecture is also a memorial to what we used to be. Buildings, having frequently proved durable beyond the most extravagant expectations of those who created them, can provide us with a wealth of clues about distant civilizations and therefore about our own collective past as well.

Is any building an example of architecture? Conventional wisdom says no. The desert island shelter hastily assembled by a lucky shipwreck survivor represents nothing more than utilitarian protection from the elements. It is unlikely to prove permanent; it has no immediate need to express any ideas about the person who erected it; and the materials used will have been determined by necessity rather than aesthetic choice. Even so, two such shelters built upon opposite sides of the same island would probably differ in minor but revealing ways. After a few weeks, all being well and no rescue ship in sight, each inhabitant might personalise his or her shelter with some improvised touches – perhaps a minor additional practical feature, a reference to home or some emblem of hope or faith. Here, perhaps, the first impulses of urban architecture begin.

In historical terms architecture seems to have begun with a handful of Neolithic settlements, most notably Jericho, some 9000 years B.C. Eleven thousand later nothing can be certain, although some sense of perspective may be gained from the fact that Jericho's archaeological discovery – and related claims that it represented one of the world's first real cities – date from the decade that also saw the rise of Elvis Presley and the election of Dwight D. Eisenhower as US President. Before the 1950s it had been assumed that Mesopotamia and its Sumerian city states of Ur, Uruk and Eridu established some 3500 years B.C., represented the earliest known cities. These issues will be explored later in this chapter, but for now it is enough to note two things. Man's first impulse to create an urban setting in which to live is at the very least 10,000 years old; and despite the fantastic variety of urban designs that have succeeded those distant civilizations of the ancient Middle East, the essential elements of the city have actually changed remarkably little.

The architecture of cities therefore reminds us that human beings of all races throughout history have made surprisingly similar demands upon their built environment.

Can architecture only exist in cities? Of course not, but the city has always been the cradle of architectural advance. It is in the context of the city that we have come to define what distinguishes architecture from other man-made structures. The word 'architecture' implies permanent buildings suitable for a variety of human activities; it also suggests the communication of ideas, emotions and experience through form. Cities large and small are where these practical demands and psychological needs have been most fully expressed and most comprehensively recorded and preserved. The city was where straightforward protection against the elements metamorphosed into a plan that brought about the creation of civilised institutions. Ultimately, it was the city as a social unit that would come to symbolise man's determination not only to survive the tangle of nature, but also – a crucial distinction – his determination to subdue it.

above & right Complex subway systems like the London Underground have been one way city developers have solved the problem of moving millions of people every day

roots

Jericho and Ain Ghazal are now known to have been settlements existing in what is present-day Jordan, at around 9000 B.C. Ain Ghazal, covering a 30-acre site, was sufficiently advanced to embrace a society that boasted art and bargaining tokens. Jericho, however, reveals more substantial signs of urban settlement. Evidence has been found of an organised community of some 2000–3000 people who, by about 8000 BC had proved themselves capable of building a huge stone wall around their town, fortified at one point by a massive tower.

Catal Hüyük

In Turkey, a shrine in Çatal Hüyük, yields a drawing resembling a town plan from around 6500 B.C. Çatal Hüyük is also the site of the first recorded religious imagery – vivid pictures of a goddess and attendants.

Three thousand years later Khirokitia in Cyprus was the site of an unwalled settlement with the apparent potential to extend itself without boundaries. It was home to about 2000 people who lived in circular, two-storey stone houses.

These and many other clues have survived the rigours the millennia. However, anyone seeking incontrovertible historical reasons as to how and why these settlements grew up when and where they did is bound to be disappointed. Assumptions and pet theories are often presented as fact, but facts tend to survive the millennia less well than fabric.

Agriculture & development

Of course, generally speaking it is reasonable to assume that exceptionally good farming conditions would create a surplus of produce, allowing self-sufficiency to be extended into commodity trading. Trade stimulates building, and sufficient building in one place stimulates urban organisation… or so the argument goes. This sequence of events is plausible, but by no means universally applicable.

Doubt arises because early experiments in urbanisation were so widely separated in space and time. The idea of any single settlement spawning all others is one that is now generally discredited. It therefore follows that any single theory as to why the city began is also likely to be too simplistic. Some argue that China, for example, never saw urban settlements as the key to taming vast tracts of land at all. There the approach was one of slow agricultural infiltration, the incremental development of a patchwork of cultivation and peasant dwellings out of which larger settlements grew very much later.

Also worth keeping in mind is the fact that prior to the recent discovery of the early settlements, it had been universally believed that the city originated in Mesopotamia, 4000 BC, spreading from there to the Indus Valley, China and westward to Greece in a slow Mexican wave of continuous urbanisation: another plausible theory discredited, reminding us that plausibility is no substitute for proof.

Mesopotamia – Greek for 'Land Between the Rivers' – made up the greater part of what is now Iraq and it certainly represented one of the most vigorous stages in the development of human civilization. A region between the Tigris and Euphrates rivers, it spawned recognisable towns, among them Ur, and, by the second millennium B.C., possibly the world's first genuine metropolis: Babylon.

stepping stones

Jericho

Any attempts to untangle the historical settlements of Jericho reveal a difficulty that recurs throughout the millennia before the birth of Christ: in this case Old Testament fables have endured rather more successfully than the archaeological evidence. Jericho is a myth in more ways than one – various settlements bearing this name are dotted throughout history.

Old Testament Jericho is marked today by a mound known as Tall As-Sultan rising some 21 metres above the surrounding plain on the west side of the Jordan River valley. Archaeologists have been anxious to discover the date of the town's destruction by the Israelites, despite most of the contemporaneous town fabric having been obliterated by erosion.

We know that there was a living town of some sort. Probably destroyed by the 14th century B.C. the site was then abandoned until the Iron Age. Archaeological excavations have established that Jericho enjoyed a long history before its biblical period. The town is synonymous with mankind's first settlements and therefore with the human race's first impulses to establish the fundamentals of the town, the city and civilised existence.

By about 8000 B.C. Jericho was the site of a community capable of building a large stone wall around itself, a wall strengthened at least at one point by a massive stone tower. The size of this settlement justifies the use of the term town and suggests a population of some 2-3000 people. It marked a movement away from hunting as a way of life to full settlement. The development of agriculture can be reasonably assumed – certainly grains of cultivated types of wheat and barley have been found. Jericho is therefore one of those sites whose expansion does seem to have been linked to the development of agriculture. It is highly probable that, in order to provide enough land for cultivation, irrigation was deployed.

The next distinct inhabitants of Jericho came in about 7000 B.C. Like that of their predecessors, theirs was another Neolithic culture but, unlike previous settlers, probably not an indigenous one. These inhabitants were travellers from other agricultural settlements to the north, and their occupancy lasted until around 6000 B.C. Little activity is subsequently recorded until the end of the 4th millennium B.C. when an urban culture once more appeared and Jericho again became a fortified town. It was to go through numerous rebuildings and redesigns over the centuries.

Jericho's subsequent history becomes increasingly fragmented, with incursions from different nomadic groups and at least three different sites all bearing the name. These culminated in a Jericho located one mile east of the Old Testament site; where the modern town eventually grew up.

above left The excavated site of Çatal Hüyük in Turkey, dating from around 6,500 B.C.

right A carved religious figure unearthed at Çatal Hüyük

Ur

The first full excavations at Ur were made shortly after World War I, through a joint expedition between the British Museum and the University of Pennsylvania.

Ur was founded during the 4th millennium B.C. by settlers from northern Mesopotamia, farmers whose culture was eventually obliterated by a major flood – in all probability the one of Biblical fame.

By 2600 B.C. the city had re-formed and a sophisticated culture had grown up, one that was extraordinarily rich in art and precious metals. This society had elaborate rituals and funeral rites in which kings were buried alongside their servants who therefore might continue in royal service after death. Excavations at a suburb of Ur named al-'Ubayd, revealed a temple sumptuously decorated with mosaics and polished copper.

However it was in Ur's 3rd Dynasty, in the 22nd and 21st centuries B.C., that a truly significant architectural achievement was created.

By that time Ur was the capital of an empire, worthy of a great monument. Its great monument was The Ziggurat.

A three-storeyed mud brick edifice faced with burnt bricks set in bitumen, The Ziggurat resembled a stepped pyramid that formed a mighty base for a small shrine to a moon god.

Its lowest stage measured 64 x 46 metres, the total height about 12 metres. Three sides rose sheer, but the fourth carried three staircases, each with 100 steps, one projecting at right angles from the middle of the building, two leaning against its wall, and all three leading to an entrance between the first and second terraces. A final single flight of steps continued up to the shrine on top. Remarkably well preserved and with adequate remains to ensure that any subsequent restoration would be highly accurate, The Ziggurat stands as clear evidence that Sumerian architects had acquired a comprehensive array of techniques more than two centuries before the birth of Christ.

They had mastered the column, the arch, the vault and the dome – nothing less than the entire fundamental vocabulary of architecture. More extraordinary still is that the Sumerians had already begun to refine these structural devices in order to create visually pleasing illusions and subtle effects. Astonishingly, the art of architecture seems to have been born simultaneously with its science.

The walls of The Ziggurat were all angled, combining with the carefully judged heights of the various stages to draw the eye upwards where the dramatic slopes of the stairways further create a focus upon the shrine itself. There are no straight lines anywhere in the structure. Everything is very slightly curved in such a way as to give an illusion of lightness instead of the sagging solidity that literal straight lines would create. This is the principle of entasis – the deliberate introduction of convexity to create visual tension. It was to be a principle famously redeployed by the builders of the Parthenon in Athens. Ur therefore exists for us today primarily as a monument not to a long forgotten deity, but to the beginnings of man's love affair with buildings. It provides evidence that the very essence of architecture – permanence, cultural importance and visual quality – was explored in the capital of a long-gone empire over 4000 years ago.

right The magnificent stone stairway leading to the top of the Ziggurat at Ur, Mesopotamia

below A full view of the Ziggurat, built to the moon god Nonna by Ur-Nommu between 2250 and 2233 B.C.

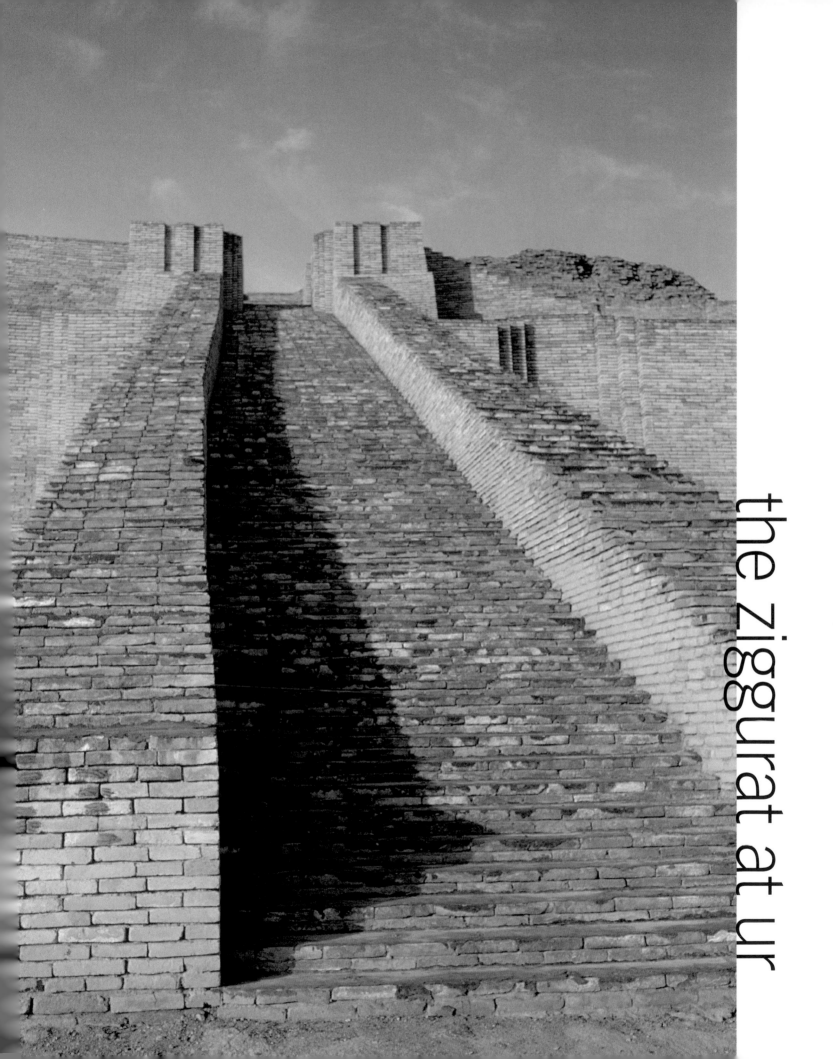

the ziggurat at ur

Memphis

According to legend, the Egyptian city of Memphis was founded about 2925 B.C. by the king Menes. The site had some obvious political advantages, being located at the junction of the boundaries of two formerly separate kingdoms. The local god of Memphis was Ptah, the patron of craftsmen and artisans, and the Great Temple of Ptah was one of Memphis' major structures.

The original name of the city was the White Wall – white being the colour of the Lower Egyptian crown – although the name probably originally referred to the king's palace with its whitewashed brick walls.

By the 3rd dynasty the importance of Memphis was fully established and its buildings left no one in any doubt that this was the pre-eminent centre of the region. Memphis' huge royal pyramid tombs stood as testimony to its greatness and marked the beginning of an extended building period of pyramids and other tomb edifices whose scale and ambition were to define the region forever.

It is worth noting that Egypt's pyramids have since become invested with such immense importance (every subsequent age's Seven Wonders of the World list, however capricious, is headed by The Pyramids) that they can be said to have served their purpose immaculately: we still know far less about Egyptian life, in the form of its cities, than we do about Egyptian death, in the form of its mighty tombs.

Djoser, the second king of the 3rd dynasty, built the Step Pyramid of Saqqarah – which was the first large monument ever to be constructed entirely of stone.

The first king of the 4th dynasty, Snefru, built two pyramid tombs at Dahshur although the three great pyramids of Giza are attributed to later 4th-dynasty monarchs. The last legitimate king of this dynasty, Shepseskaf, built his tomb at South Saqqarah. This was not a pyramid but a distinctive oblong structure with sloping sides, later named the Mastabat Fir'awn.

The royal pyramids are surrounded by large cemeteries where, once again, the courtiers and officials who had served the king during his lifetime were buried. The reliefs discovered in some of these tombs include scenes of daily life and give some insights into the crafts, costumes, and lifestyle of the royal court of Memphis.

The kings of the 5th dynasty (c. 2465–c. 2325) moved south of Giza to build their funerary monuments. Their pyramids, at Abu Sir, are much smaller than those of the 4th dynasty, but the auxiliary temples and causeways were decorated with exceptionally fine reliefs. The decline of Memphis continued for centuries, and our relatively scant knowledge of its architectural accomplishments – other than those reflected in its famous monuments – seem forever to have cast Memphis as the city of kings and triumphant memorials. Babylon was to yield different clues.

Babylon

Babylon's development as a major city came late by Mesopotamian standards. After the fall of the 3rd dynasty of Ur, Babylon became the focus of a small kingdom established in 1894 B.C. by the Amorite king Sumuabum, whose descendants gradually consolidated its status. By the 6th Amorite dynasty (1792-50 B.C.), the rulers of Babylon had conquered most of the surrounding city-states and had made Babylon the capital of a wide range of territories.

Babylon had become the capital of southern Mesopotamia – also known as Babylonia – from the early 2nd millennium B.C. This was the Babylon of Nebuchadrezzar I (1124-03) and it became the largest city in the world, covering 2500 acres and focussed upon the central temple of Marduk and its associated ziggurat Etemenanki, now identified forever in Biblical mythology as the Tower of Babel.

Mythology still surrounds our perceptions of Babylon today. It has passed into contemporary thought variously as a place of sad exile, a vague synonym for corruption, the Biblical symbol of man's chronic inability to communicate with his neighbour and the site of one of another of the Seven Wonders of The World. All of this diverts attention away from the more concrete fact that from about 1790–1750 B.C. the city of Babylon had come to represent a watershed in urban development, providing a highly recognisable model for all cities that would follow.

In its way Babylon was even more impressive than Ur. It was situated in a fertile river basis in an area where major trade routes coincided. In addition the Tigris and Euphrates rivers were themselves major routes for

left The entrance to the Step Pyramid complex of Saqqarah, in Memphis, Egypt

below The fabled Hanging Gardens of Babylon, here in an illustration c.1700, which in fact formed the Ziggurat of the Babylonian capital city

the transport of valuable timber. However, even these benign circumstances might not have been enough to generate sophisticated urban development had it not been for yet another historical factor.

The need to maximise food production for a growing population had necessitated the construction of a network of irrigation canals. Building this network in turn demanded the development of technological skills and specialised equipment. Once these existed the Babylonians found that they also had at their disposal the technical means to enclose their city, thereby securing greater comfort and protection whilst simultaneously creating an enclosed urban unit that would therefore be naturally inclined to develop its own internal rules and regulations – the defining accompaniment to civilised living.

Babylon was very much a planned city, and it was planned for effect and psychological impact as well as habitability.

Babylon's famous ziggurat boasted seven levels, culminating in a blue glaze temple at a height of 90 metres. This was not the only temple in Babylon – archaeologists have discovered four others in the eastern part of the city, and contemporary records indicate that still more existed.

East and west sides of the city were separated by the river Euphrates and joined by a bridge built on brick piles. So here, almost two centuries before the birth of Christ, we find a model for a familiar urban layout that can today be seen in hundreds of cities worldwide, from Memphis, Tennessee to Paris, London and Cologne: the lifeblood of the river feeds two settlements, one on either bank, and these two centres of activity are subsequently connected by a bridge.

Along the Euphrates river, especially in the local region of Esagila on the eastern side of the city, existed substantial numbers of warehouses and quays, evidence that trade flourished. Other city features familiar today could also be found in Babylon. For example, the streets were laid out on a grid, with the main axis parallel to the river. A celebratory thoroughfare was built, the Processional Way, and this passed through the highly decorated – and highly fortified – Ishtar Gate, culminating at a temple technically outside the city proper. West of the Ishtar Gate, one of eight city gates lay two well-protected palace complexes that covered about 40 acres with their fortifications.

To the east of the Processional Way lay a long-established zone of private dwellings disposed around central courtyards.

Fortification was crucial to Babylon. Walls and ditches encircled both east and west sides of the city. Beyond those walls to the east a 10-mile outer rampart met the river bank north and south of the city.

Situated between these inner and outer defences lay the ancient network of canals whose original construction had laid the groundwork for the technology and building skills that created the city.

The origin of Babylon's famous Hanging Gardens remains ambiguous. Like the Tower of Babel, the potency of the legend is rather better developed than the historical evidence. In subsequent Hellenistic times there was reference to a synthesized hill of terracing planted with vegetation and covering a vaulted substructure of some sort. This Hellenistic historians deemed one of the Seven Wonders of the World.

below Pont Neuf in Paris; the bridge became the architectural link between previously separate communities, allowing cities to grow

right The state-connecting Mississippi Bridge running from Memphis, Tennessee to West Memphis in neighbouring Arkansas

Recent archaeologists claim to have discovered the base of this structure within the palace complex. However, a rival theory maintains that the Ziggurat and the Hanging Gardens were one and the same, the Ziggurat itself being richly planted with trees.

city limits

Myths, legends and ambiguous relics. If one thing alone is clear from our knowledge of mankind's earliest settlements, it is the fact that our knowledge is necessarily incomplete. Archaeologists and historians are in the business of reconstruction and interpretation, and the fact that they have managed to unearth and decipher so much, cannot obscure the fact that we still have no more than a few fascinating glimpses into mankind's urban beginnings in the East. It may well be that the rapid continuing development of modern technologies – as well as the ever-present possibility of new and unexpected archaeological finds – means that we may yet discover more hard evidence that will lead to a much fuller understanding of the origins of the city.

However, for now, the 'meanings' of Jericho, Ur, Babylon and infinite numbers of smaller settlements, are necessarily muffled by the vast stretches of time that separate us from them. What can we safely infer about the birth of the city? Can we do more than guess at the societies that produced them? Do those proto-towns leave us enough evidence to define them as genuine cities by today's standards? If not, what exactly does define a city in the earliest historical sense?

In response one can say that perhaps it does not do to be too literal in these matters. For our purposes, it is safe to assume that what gave rise to cities was a human impulse to form and celebrate a society. That impulse was probably always there, but only when a happy coincidence of geography, climate, history and most of all technology, brought them together at the right time, did man's ambition for society – that is for the permanence, security and inclusiveness of an organised urban existence – start to find practical expression. That expression was the settlement, the town, the city.

The rudimentary city was a phenomenon destined to repeat itself unevenly, fitfully and often in historical isolation for many centuries. Only gradually did those fragmented urban settlements assume their place in a more logical, linear perspective of human history. That they should have done so was inevitable. Bigger and better civilizations came into being, and these were always mindful of the past as they created what was to become the classical foundation of architecture. From the start those who shaped the great civilizations of antiquity referred to the architecture of their predecessors. They wanted to incorporate the best of the past into their own vision of the future. In doing so they established architecture as nothing less than the prime symbol and expression of the continuity of human progress.

2

greek cities
& hellenism

The Asklepieion, Kos

links with the past

Today the cities of the classic Greek civilization are universally seen as the true starting point of European urban development – the beginning of the city form as we today find it most recognisable and comprehensible. At first glance these Greek city states may look to have sprung fully formed, evidence of a superior civilization that was simultaneously original, innovative and supremely self-confident. They certainly have all the hallmarks of being very specifically shaped environments created for the sole purpose of reflecting the sophisticated spiritual, intellectual and aesthetic impulses that ancient Greece developed, advanced and ultimately embodied.

In fact the Greeks, who were to exert an immeasurable influence on all who followed, were themselves very much influenced by their own region's past and the heritage of the bronze age. Inveterate borrowers and adapters, the Greeks are more usually celebrated as originators. In fact, of course, they were both.

Crete

The first major civilization to be founded in Europe had developed on the island of Crete; this civilization is frequently referred to as Minoan (after the probably mythical king Minos of Knossos which was the chief city of Crete in early times).

Founded around 5000 B.C. this Cretan civilization endured until the mid-second century B.C. and was distinguished with many palaces constructed of mud bricks, plaster and rubble. Its defining characteristic was a dedication to what we would now call 'quality of life'. After the fortified cities of the past and the Egyptian preoccupation with building for

below left Part of the elaborate domestic arrangements evident in the Minoan palaces of Crete

below The Minoan Palace at Knossos, built between 1900 and 1700 B.C., destroyed in 1375 B.C. and excavated and reconstructed in 1900

right Interior of the Knossos palace showing clearly the columns lining the stairwell and the frescoed walls

knossos

the dead, the civilization that grew up on Crete seems to have been more concerned with living, comfort and culture than with war and immortality.

Protected by the sea – and therefore with its defensive power residing almost exclusively in its naval strength rather than its built environment – Crete built palaces that were decorated with frescoes and richly appointed with furnished rooms, courtyards and cloisters, sophisticated drainage systems, elaborate provisions for subterranean food storage, charcoal heating systems and, in the case of the main palace at Knossos, a grand columnar staircase, the first ever recorded.

Cretan civilization offered a seductive model, and not only to the Greeks. Because of its natural island defences Crete's architecture was left to respond to human needs in a more relaxed and reflective way, without the physical and psychological constraints of fortification. It did so in an apparently relaxed spirit of hedonism, and various mainland peoples eventually adapted to their own ends what they found to be the most appealing elements of Cretan civilization, and its architecture in particular.

Meanwhile on the mainland at Mycenae, on the plain of Argos, there had grown up a centre of culture parallel to that of Crete. Its remains date from about 1300 B.C., and in character it was obviously very different from Crete. Heavily fortified, Mycenae and its neighbouring towns of Tiryns and Pylos variously reflected the ethos of its warrior rulers who, in all probability, were those responsible for invading Crete, appropriating its trade and terminating its civilization by about 1400 B.C.

Mycenae

Unlike that of Knossos, the archaeological evidence bequeathed by the mainland is very fragmentary and our knowledge of Mycenaean architecture dates largely from what is known as the Late Helladic period (1580 to c. 1100 B.C.).

The remains of palaces have been discovered at Mycenae, Tiryns, Pylos, Gla, and Phylakopi. The palace at Pylos shows a typical plan containing four elements: a court at the front of the structure; a twin column entrance portico; a vestibule; and a frescoed main hall complete with throne and a central hearth beneath an open structure rising above the roof to give light and ventilation. Some of Mycenae's private dwellings were appointed with very similar features suitably reduced in scale.

However the region's most energetic building programme of the 14th century B.C. was very much a response to the militaristic spirit of the age. Fortresses were built in key positions and featured some colossal defensive elements. Vast rudimentary walls of rough, untrimmed stone

above The celebrated Lion Gate at Mycenae (c.1350–1330 B.C.) with its revolutionary structure plain to see

blocks were built simply by fitting them together without mortar and trusting to bulk and weight for stability.

The fragmentary and dislocated nature of early architectural history is once again illustrated by the fact that the Mycenaeans apparently had no knowledge of the arch, a form that had already been elegantly employed at Ur a thousand years before.

However, the famous Lion Gate at Mycenae is an epic piece of architectural invention that consists of two posts supporting a monolithic lintel. This gate clearly demanded an equivalent of the arch to support the heavy wall above, and the Mycenaeans solved the problem by constructing the appropriate section of wall in a way that formed a relieving triangle above the lintel. This triangular space was then filled with a relief panel featuring the two lions from which the gate takes its name.

A closely related structure to this stress-relieving device is the corbel vault. This consists of rows of masonry arranged so that each new row projects slightly beyond the one below. Two such opposing arrangements then meet at the top to form a false arch. The corbel arch makes its first appearance in mainland Europe in the concealed galleries of Tiryns.

Early royal burial chambers in Mycenae could hardly be said to have rivalled the grandeur of the pyramids, consisting as they did of little more than vertical shafts cut into the bedrock – a concept closer to waste disposal than any celebration of immortality. Considerably more interesting are the family sepulchres of which the finest example is the Treasury of Atreus (also known as the Tomb of Agamemnon) at Mycenae. It is one of the most prominent monuments of the city being a pointed dome constructed of corbeled blocks of masonry cut and polished to give the impression of a genuine vault. Another lintel, similar to that of the Lion Gate, uses the same triangular relief device.

By about 1100 B.C., and probably as the result of invasion, Mycenae's culture was obliterated. Its buildings were destroyed by fire, its treasures plundered, its population dispersed. Following this, some 3 or 400 years of poverty and savagery replaced the former period of enlightenment. Then came an early sign of a cultural renaissance. What was to become Hellenistic culture was heralded by the appearance of a form of writing based upon that used in Mycenae.

hellenism

The reintroduction of a written language was the signal of a revival of cultural fortunes which, to begin with, had no clear focus. Unlike many previous cultures, Hellenic culture was for centuries more a state of mind than any well-defined geographical plot. Because of the irregular coastal landscape and many ethnic differences, the population of Greece was geographically diffused and roughly divided between the Ionians and the Dorians, each of which cultures gave rise to some distinctive cities of its own. The Ionians founded Athens (previously a Mycenaen town), Eretria and Massalia, the forerunner of Marseilles. The Dorians founded Sparta, Corinth, Thebes and Argos and also established settlements on Crete, Corfu and Rhodes. These two distinct but eventually complementary strands of Greek culture co-existed separately until 179 B.C. when the final suppression of their main rivals (the Persians and Phonecians) served to draw them together in a closer alliance of city states. These city states still had many differences, but in triumph against common enemies, largely due to the efforts of Alexander the Great, they also discovered a common cultural purpose. Hellenistic architecture was a style that developed in parallel with and persisted longer than classical Greek architecture, always favouring a more sculptural and decorative ethos and primarily focused upon Alexandria, a city whose grid plan layout and vast buildings have not survived the centuries. Many of the most impressive Hellenistic buildings were civic, notably the Bouleterion at Miletus and the later additions to Athens' agora. Domestic dwellings reprised something of the emphasis placed upon them at Mycenae, although – no doubt in deference to the legacy of Alexander the Great – military aggrandizement in buildings flourished too, often beyond practical needs. Forts, walls and triumphant arches survive in parts of Greece and Asia Minor, notably Priene.

Despite its fragmentary nature Hellenism endured and ultimately even survived Roman conquest, providing, in the process, a recognisable link between Greece and Rome.

greece

Until the Classical period the Greek architect's main role was to design religious buildings. The altar, originally just a simple block, stood in the open air. If a temple existed, the altar usually stood to the east of it. The temple was basically a house for the deity whose presence was represented within by a statue. Various devices were employed to distinguish temples from houses. To begin with temples were given elongated plans so that the statue could be viewed from a distance beyond a row of central pillar supports. Externally, a colonnade of posts (or peristyle) supported extended eaves. This arrangement can be seen in buildings on Samos and at Thermum. The construction was extremely simple: rubble and mud brick, with timbering and a thatched or flat clay roof. By about 700 B.C. the development of roof tiles made a lower pitched roof possible, and later, fired clay facings were being made to decorate and protect the vulnerable wooden upper sections of buildings.

From about 650 B.C. onwards, the Greeks began to visit Egypt where they came across the huge stone buildings that were to inspire and influence the development of monumental architecture and sculpture in Greece. To begin with this process involved little more than re-inventing brick and wood forms as stone equivalents. However, this process of transposition also offered new opportunity for the application of expressive detail. It was this detail that would eventually lead to the evolution of the stone 'orders' of architecture. These orders, or arrangements of columns supporting an upper section called an entablature, defined the pattern of the columnar facades and upperworks that formed the basic decorative shell of the Greek temple building.

The Doric temple evolved towards the end of the 7th century B.C. and it was to become the single most lasting achievement of Greek

Vaults & Domes

A vault is an arched roof or ceiling made out of brick or stone. Many different variations exist, of which the most common are: Tunnel, Groin, Rib, Fan. A dome is a vault that is evenly curved and built upon a circular base. Domes, like vaults, evolved from the arch, and in their simplest form they may be considered as a series of arches with a common central point. A dome exerts thrusts all around its perimeter, and so, in all of its earliest forms, demanded heavy walls which had to be more or less round or to give continuous support. This was the chief reason why it could be so difficult to incorporate the dome into complex buildings.

Additionally, putting a dome on top of a square base – a logical requirement, since most buildings tend to be rectilinear – required further ingenuity. Even so, throughout architectural history, the simpler option of vaulting has often given way to the superior emotional impact of the dome. Even in the early industrial era construction, many buildings retained masonry domes without exploiting the new advantages of iron and steel. Rare 19th century exceptions to this rule include the Halle aux Blés, Paris and the Coal Exchange, London. The concept of the 'false' dome has generally more to do with traditional models – for example Florence Cathedral and St. Paul's Cathedral, London utilize an internal shell constructed on the same foundations to minimize the visual effect of a tunnel-like depth created by the external dome.

In modern times new materials and pre-fabricated elements like curved concrete slabs have made traditional distinctions between vaults and domes redundant. Meanwhile the geodesic dome, developed in the 20th century by R. Buckminster Fuller, is a freestanding form in which light skeletal struts or flat planes replace the arch principle altogether.

Doric

The Doric (above left) order was invented in the second half of the 7th century. Its parts – the simple, baseless columns, the spreading capitals, and the patterned frieze above the columns – were an aesthetic reworking in stone of themes used in earlier wood and brick construction. Doric remained the favourite order of the Greek mainland and western colonies, and it changed remarkably little throughout its history. Early examples, such as the temple at Thermum, were not completely made of stone and incorporated large amounts of much timber and some fired clay.

Ionic

The Ionic order (centre) evolved later, in eastern Greece. About 600 BC, at Smyrna, the first intimation of the style appeared in stone columns with capitals elaborately carved in floral hoops – an Oriental style of pattern familiar mainly on smaller objects and furniture and, to all intents and purposes, simply magnified for the purposes of buildings. This hoop pattern was to be the characteristic element in the full development of the Ionic order.

Corinthian

The Corinthian capital (right) was shaped like an upturned bell surrounded by detailed sculptured leaves, and had the advantage over the Ionic order that corner pillars could be viewed from any side – the Ionic was designed to be viewed from the front. The flamboyant symmetry made possible in the Corinthian order was very popular in the later lavish design excesses of the Roman Empire.

architecture. Essentially the Doric temple was bold and simple in design, with a harmonious look and a use of decoration that accentuated its lines without camouflaging them. The earliest surviving Doric temple is the Temple of Hera at Olympia, built sometime before 600 B.C. It was an example of a wooden columnar building being gradually refurbished with stone columns. Another temple from the same period, in Korkyra on Corfu, shows that already sculptures were being applied to the pediments.

Early Doric temples were often equipped with columns that look rather crude, although this is at least in part due to the fact that their covering of smooth stucco has disappeared. A more elegant temple was that of Hephaistos in Athens built around 450 B.C.

The Hellenistic period spanned the 4th and 1st centuries B.C. and followed a successful period of expansion for the area that we now call Greece, largely due to widespread military successes. It was during the Hellenistic period the Greeks on the mainland began to introduce a strong social element into town life, the result of their preoccupation with the concept of democracy. It was one of the most important architectural developments of all time, this democratic need for widespread consultation, public assembly for the purposes of decision-making and debate, and it conditioned town-planning in a fundamental way. Religious meeting places were well enough established, but now came a real appetite for secular meeting areas. Primarily took the form of the agora – a spacious bordered area, centrally situated, in which citizens might exchange views, resolve problems and hold discussions. The agora combined the practical with the symbolic – always a key function of serious architecture – and whilst the agora was initially little more than a space (a piece of town planning rather than a building) it did come to acquire various architectural additions during the Classical Period. Bordered on at least one side by a colonnade designed to provide shelter from the elements, the agora gradually became more of an enclosure. The agora at Priene, for example, was totally enclosed by colonnades, providing the kind of powerful central space that attracted traders and artisans often acquired extra built elements like theatres, fountains, weathercocks and sun dials. There is a clear parallel, in character and ambience if not in specific purpose, with many of today's cities' shopping malls, leisure centres and large public spaces such as Centre Pompidou in Paris, Covent Garden in London or Faneuil Hall in Boston. The Greeks very much favoured an external, open-air aesthetic. Not only were the market place and the agora by definition external spaces, but one of the Greeks' most influential building types, the temple, also concentrated its effects on the exterior although it need not have done.

The Greek temple, of which the Doric form was to remain the dominant one, was defined according to three distinct styles or orders: Doric, Ionic and later Corinthian. The famous visual clues for distinguishing between them are given by the decoration at the top of the supporting columns, and often these clear distinctions are taken as evidence of the Greeks' originality in creating buildings with such identifiable features. However, subtler visual clues reveal that the Greeks were just as keen to appropriate from the past as to innovate for the future. Underlying the Greek temple as a more general building type were the primitive structures of the Egyptians who had used bound reeds to make supporting columns, topping them with functional blocks of wood to support the roof structure. Thus the 'classic', 'pure' fluted columns of the Greeks can be seen as intentionally stylized re-inventions of an earlier technique, using newer (or at least different) technology whilst playfully referring to now redundant architectural techniques from the past. Incidentally, neither can we assume, as generations did, that the elegant, bleached ruins of Greece visible today always looked that way. When the French architect Jacques-Ignace Hittorff (who built the Gare du Nord in Paris) published his impressions of what Greek temples might have looked like with their original multi-coloured décor, he destroyed that myth forever in the popular imagination and, incidentally, paved the way for all manner of Victorian decorative excess. Yet another common misconception is that Greek temples were exclusively stone edifices. To begin with wood was used almost exclusively and persisted later as a roofing material (a fact which offers a likely explanation as to why the ruins of Greek temples are usually roofless. However stone roofs also occurred and were certainly prevalent in the Hellenistic period.

high classical period

What we now think of as Greece's High Classical period occurred in the second half of the 4th century B.C. By this time Greek culture had reached its peak and its architecture strongly reflected this. The progression of Doric temples had led to a particularly elegant one in the shape of the temple of Hephaistos in Athens. The finest pieces of Greek architecture of this period – perhaps the finest ever built in any period by anyone – were built on the orders of Pericles and were also located in Athens and centred on the Acropolis, the natural focus of the city. Rising 152 metres above sea level and with a solitary natural approach, the Acropolis promised drama and excitement that had throughout history made it a natural location for architectural fortifications and memorials. Under Pericles it was to see its finest hour as the setting for a temple of eternal elegance, simplicity and art. The Parthenon demonstrates better than any other Greek building the immense sophistication of the culture that produced it. Everything about it suggests a view of the world in which stability and permanence coexisted with a deference to higher spiritual forces.

above A reconstructed impression of a High Classic Greek temple by Jacques-Ignace Hittorff which shows the bright multi-coloured decor

the acropolis and
the parthenon

The Parthenon

Designed by the architect Ictinus, the Parthenon is of more stately design than most Doric temples. Here deployed with an eight-column façade instead of the usual six, the Doric temple style might have been thought to run the risk of producing a rather stolid building. It was this danger that Ictinus managed to avoid by replacing a rigid geometrical accuracy with subtly distorted lines.

In keeping with the Greeks' preoccupations with the psychological effects of external spaces, most of the architectural effects of the Parthenon were concentrated in the exterior of the building. The interior formed a shrine to the goddess Athena (from whom the city of Athens took its name), forming a shelter rather than a functioning place of public worship. Accordingly, it was the outside that bore the load of making a strong visual impression.

The building's now legendary visual lightness was chiefly accomplished by the avoidance of any lines or verticals that were perfectly straight in the surrounding colonnade. Each vertical is slightly curved. The columns, of reduced thickness toward the centre of the colonnade and set progressively closer together, lean toward the building's centre. Even the flutings of the individual columns diminish in width as they rise. These visual *tours de force* are virtually imperceptible to the casual eye but together combine to achieve that sense of lightness and weightlessness that epitomizes the Greek obsession with leavening structural solidity through psychological manipulation.

It also plays its part in a remarkable complex which makes imaginative and contrasting use of the orders.

The ensemble of major buildings – the Parthenon itself, temple to Athena; the Erechtheum , housing its various cults; and the monumental Propylaea, gateway to the Acropolis – demonstrates how these orders could be made to work together effectively.

The Erechtheum offers decorative Ionic relief to the sterner Doric lines of the Parthenon. Meanwhile in the Propylaea, columns drawn from both orders exist quite happily side by side.

The importance of civic pride and a sense of active citizenship is reflected in the Erechtheum's frieze which depicts the procession of citizens in an annual festival held in honour of Athena.

The Erechtheum was in fact a far more complex architectural undertaking than the Parthenon. Built on an irregular site, it was also a building intended to celebrate several different cults, which meant it required three porches and three different floor levels. The Erechtheum's Caryatid porch, with its use of female figures as columns, derives from an Oriental motif familiar from Delphi.

The Propylaea was designed by Mnesicles, who had to adapt the rigid conventions of colonnade construction to a steeply rising site.

The Parthenon incorporated other buildings too, but it is these three that represented the absolute summation of classic Greek design, innovation and subtlety of thought. No barbarian state could have envisaged them let alone created them, even if they had been given unlimited materials and labour.

above The Six Maidens, the female figures used as columns in the Caryatid porch of the Erechtheum

left A view of the Acropolis with the Propylaea gateway and the Erechtheum visible to the left of the all-dominant Parthenon

below The Ionic columns of the Temple of Nike Apteros (the Wingless Victory), the oldest surviving building in the Acropolis

Athens

The Parthenon and its complementary buildings represent the very best that Greek culture and Greek architecture could achieve at their peak. Greek architecture was not, however, limited to a dazzling cluster of buildings on a single Athenian hilltop. Several new Doric temples were also built in the lower city of Athens and in the Attic countryside, the Ionic order generally being reserved for the smaller temples. Even though Ionic was never used as the exterior order for a major building on the Greek mainland, Athens did add some new forms of column base to the order.

Gradually the use of the orders was no longer limited to temple buildings. In the marketplace at Athens various public buildings appeared in which the orders were applied to structures of varying designs and function: the portico of a colonnade, a council house, and a circular meeting house for state officials. Even the buildings attached to the flat circular orchestra of the theatre started to absorb the monumental look, suggesting perhaps a filtering down of architectural grandeur from lofty temple to the quotidian structure.

In fact the finest of Athens' secular buildings were its great theatres, particularly the theatre of Dionysus in the shadow of the Acropolis. Constructed in the 5th century B.C. this was subsequently much altered. The theatre of Epidaurus from around 350 B.C. was also notable, not just because of its visual elegance but also for its surprising technical command of acoustics.

Athens also had an agora and on its approaches there still stands an unusually well-preserved temple from the 5th century B.C. Almost completely intact, this temple, known as the Theseum, offers a useful correctional reminder to those who, having noted that Greece was capable of creating buildings of great beauty, mistakenly assume that it was incapable of creating any other sort. The Theseum, built by unknown architects, lacks all the grace and beauty of the Acropolis buildings.

Nor was the Acropolis the only commanding hill upon which dramatic buildings were tried. Across Apostólou Pávlou (Apostle Paul Avenue) stand three other hills: the Hill of the Nymphs, where a 19th century baron would one day build an observatory; the Hill of the Muses, surmounted by the remains of the marble monument to Philopappus, a Roman consul of the 2nd century A.D.; and the middle hill, the Pnyx, the celebrated meeting place of the Ecclesia, where, in theory at least, up to 15,000 citizens could gather to hear the great orators of the day.

Athens also boasted the Horologium. The eight-sided, 12 metre-high marble structure was known as the Tower of the Winds because figures representing the wind from different compass points stand on each of its sides. Once equipped with a sundial, a water clock for telling the time on sunless days, and a weather vane, the Horologium was left unscathed by the Turks who mistakenly believed it to be the tomb of Socrates and Plato.

Mainland Greece

After Athens, which it could never match for architectural elegance, Delphi was one of the most important Greek centres and the location of the major ancient Greek temple and oracle of Apollo. This was situated on a steep lower slope of Mount Parnassus, about six miles from the Gulf of Corinth and considered by the ancient Greeks to be nothing less than the centre of the world. According to legend, Zeus released two eagles, one from the east, the other from the west, and when they met at Delphi, the spot was marked by a stone in the temple; this stone was known as the omphalos.

Colourful legend aside, Delphi was also the site of a marble tholos (a conically-roofed round building of uncertain ceremonial purpose) built in 370 B.C. Highly ornamented and rich in careful detail, the tholos was adorned on the exterior by a Doric colonnade and contained a circle of ten Corinthian columns.

A larger tholos at Epidaurus took 30 years to construct, from 360 B.C. to 330 B.C., and offers a further example of the development of the Corinthian order. Here 14 Corinthian columns circled the interior and revealed delicately-detailed carvings featuring the now familiar stylized acanthus leaves.

The tholos is generally thought to have been the main vehicle for advancing the influence of the Corinthian order, and the Hellenistic-influenced building form was to find its most fanciful expression in The Choragic Monument of Lysicrates, to be discussed in the following section.

towards an architecture

Stylistically speaking, the main achievement of Greek architecture was the development of the Doric temple, of which the Parthenon remains the pinnacle. Towards the end of Greece's architectural development, the influence of Hellenism – that decorative and geographically fragmented reworking of Greece's own past – became more marked and the trend was towards ornamentation a more self-conscious elegance, usually incorporating the Corinthian order.

The Choragic Monument of Lysicrates typifies this final phase. Erected in honour of victory at Dionysia, the structure is a complex one with a 3-metre square foundation supporting a 6-metre high circular marble building itself topped by a circular structure supported on six Corinthian columns. A frieze depicts Tyrrhenian pirates being turned into dolphins by the god Dionysius, a naval manoeuvre of the sort that tends to be more plausible on celebratory friezes than in the heat of battle.

left The classic, and best-known, of all Greek classical buildings, the Parthenon (470-432 B.C.), which has dominated the Acropolis to this day

below A detail from the marble northern frieze of the Parthenon, showing a procession of horsemen

It is perhaps no coincidence that the fulsome aesthetic typified by the Choragic Monument found great favour in the 18th century. By the time of its construction, the Greeks' finest architectural hour was behind them – although it would seem unreasonable to expect them to have extended such levels of achievement indefinitely.

When the 20th century Swiss architect Le Corbusier gave the title *Towards An Architecture* to one of his pieces of theoretical writing, he was simply putting a name to an ongoing process that the Greeks had all but invented. The phrase sounds more awkward in English than French, but its central idea – that of the evolution of ideas about buildings leading towards some sort of rational approach – is one which the Greeks could have fairly claimed to have begun. Credited by later generations with much originality that they did not deserve, the Greeks did in fact initiate something of immense innovative importance to the civilised world: the search for eternally valid rules of form and proportion.

The Greeks sought to create buildings that related to human beings and an orderly civic process, whilst simultaneously celebrating spirituality and divinities that by definition exceeded human scale. They were moving towards a classically ideal architecture. Their achievement has never been exceeded, and today the battered Parthenon still stands, now well into its third millennium and still performing its extraordinary hilltop feat of monumental weightlessness.

Plutarch wrote of the Parthenon and its accompanying buildings: 'They were created in a short time for all time. Each in its fineness was even then age-old; but in the freshness of its vigour it is, even to the present day, recent and newly-wrought'.

This remains as good a summary as has ever been offered.

a change of emphasis

In Athens at around 175 B.C., below the Acropolis the great Olympeion began construction. It was the first truly grand Corinthian building, offering a lively contrast to the timeless and sober buildings above. Under different historical circumstances, this might have marked the beginning of another stage in Athenian and Greek culture.

However Greek civilisation was nearing its end. Despite its extraordinary temples, public buildings and grand public spaces Athens had been slowly declining since the 3rd century B.C.

The Athenian empire had been weakened by the Peloponnesian War against Sparta which state had latterly enjoyed support from Persia. A military defeat for Athens in 406 B.C. effectively brought to an end the city's supremacy and with it Greece's stability as a whole. Athens' fortunes had always been somewhat unstable due to its intermittent success or failure in various military conflicts, and gradually, in terms of everyday living, uncertainty and lack of confidence was reflected in the city fabric which failed to change with the times. Latterly Athens suffered from an out-of-date town plan with narrow and winding streets, having antiquated services and a notoriously hard water supply.

Meanwhile the victorious Persian/ Spartan alliance had proved short-lived, Alexander the Great having destroyed it around 340 B.C. and replaced it with a Near East empire that drew heavily upon the influence of Greece which it reinvented as the mature phase of Hellenism. Three principal Hellenistic kingdoms existed: the Ptolemaic kingdom of Egypt; the Antigonid kingdom of Macedon; and the Seleucid kingdom of Syria.

It was to be Hellenism, a fragmented series of civilisations that first echoed and then influenced the culture of mainland Greece, that provided the natural link to the next great civilisation. Hellenistic temples might still use the classic Greek Doric temple form, but the columns were becoming more slender, and increasingly motifs from the Ionic order were being introduced by 175 B.C.

Finally, in 86 B.C. Athens was captured by the Roman general Sulla. This conquest saw wholesale slaughter and total destruction of private houses, but the only public building destroyed was the Odeum of Pericles. This was burned by the defenders to prevent its timbers being used by the invaders.

left The best-preserved of all Greek amphitheatres, built in the 3rd Century B.C. at Epidaurus

right The Temple of Apollo built by the Greeks at Didyma, which is located in present-day Turkey

temple of apollo, didyma

rome:republic
& empire

Pont du Gard, Provence

the rising empire

As Greece diminished in power, Rome continued to flourish, progressing through its early and late Republics and demonstrating a unique combination of military might, ruthlessness and fascination with culture. In time it would eventually develop into an Empire that would provide an enduring model for the cyclical nature of all future civilisations. The Romans' architectural achievements would be outstanding in themselves, building as they did upon the cumulative knowledge of contemporaries and predecessors, most notably the Greeks. However, they instigated some significant advances too.

The Glory of Rome would be the glory of military success underpinned by an insatiable appetite for culture, order and civic grandeur. Most of all, the cities of The Roman Empire would be a matrix of urban centres shaped and determined in almost every detail by politics.

In the 3rd and 2nd centuries B.C. Rome's military might had ensured that it and not Carthage would become the controller of the Western World. Its military power subjugated a vast swathe of territories: Greece, Macedonia, Carthage and its North African territories, Corinth, Athens, Syria and by 30 B.C., Egypt. The territories that would make up the Roman Empire were vast and our knowledge of Roman architecture comes mainly from remains that are scattered far and wide throughout those many areas that became part of that Empire. Some remains are merely fragments and some are comparatively well-preserved, and others can only be assessed through theoretical restoration.

However Roman writings have filled in many of the blanks in our knowledge, and none more so than the classic ten-book treatise on architecture by Vitruvius, *De architectura*. Written around 27 B.C. *De architectura* dealt with almost every aspect of contemporary Roman architecture of the period preceding the Empire.

In addition, the prolific Roman libraries contained everything from economic records and legal treatises to dramatic texts and philosophical works. Many of these works have come down to us over the centuries and greatly expanded our understanding of the Romans' relationship with building and town planning.

The protracted period of military expansion leading up to and beyond the life of Christ had naturally brought immense material wealth from the conquered territories. The Romans therefore had quite literally an embarrassment of riches with which to create monuments to themselves and their achievements. These would be monuments to eclipse everything that had gone before. Since much of what had gone before was now literally in Roman hands, quite a lot of it could be used as raw material for these new living monuments – cities conceived and organised on a scale sufficiently ambitious and grandiose to reflect the importance of the new Empire. Rome itself was to be the greatest monument of all.

a living monument

The Romans succeeded in creating their living monument not least because their building skills were at their zenith. No amount of triumphal ambition would have brought about the Glory of Rome had its architects and builders not been capable of mastering the complex constructions and building techniques.

Just before the birth of Christ, Rome had been ambitiously redeveloped in a manner that prefigured today's city overspill programmes. The Emperor Gaius Julius Caesar (100 – 44 B.C.) understood, like many since, that life was getting unacceptably crowded in the city and so began strategically to develop new areas for expansion, initially buying up large plots of land next to the Forum Romanum. A second Forum – the Forum Caesarum – was duly constructed there. Yet another large citizens' assembly was created on the Martian Field. This redevelopment programme also marked the beginning of the long process of turning Rome from a timber-built city into a more permanent one characterised by marble facings and fine tiles. Gaius Julius Caesar did not live to see his work completed but the Emperor Augustus continued his predecessor's redevelopment plan and also issued a declaration that the wealthy must effectively be taxed to fund major civic buildings. Sometimes this tax was direct, in the sense that the wealthy were expected to fund specific

left A reconstruction of the city of Rome as it was at the time of the Emperor Septimius Severus, who ruled from 193 to 211 A.D.

above right The magificent Roman Forum as it appears today, with the Colosseum visible in the background

forum romanum

The Forum Romanum

The Forum Romanum was the original centre of social life in Rome. A small, closed valley surrounded by the Seven Hills, the Forum included, at one end of the valley, two meeting places, one for political meetings and one for social gatherings. Each had shops down both sides. At the opposite end of the valley was the precinct of the high priest next to the keepers of the sacred flame. In between were temples of the gods.

De architectura

Marcus Vitruvius Pollio was an architect of no particular significance as a practitioner, who lived at about the same time as Christ. He had served under Julius Caesar in the African War of 46 B.C. and, as an architect, seemed to have more personal allegiance to the Hellenistic building principles of the past than to those of the burgeoning Roman Empire. In old age he wrote *De architectura* which was based partly on his own experience and partly on the work of notable Greek architects. His now legendary ten-part treatise covers almost every aspect of contemporary architecture, although was somewhat retrospective in spirit even when it was written; Vitruvius is perhaps the first commentator on record to mutter darkly about the lamentable quality of 'modern architecture'.

The ten books deal with city planning and architecture; building materials; temple construction and the use of the Greek orders; public buildings; private buildings; floors and stucco decoration; hydraulics; clocks, the principles of measurement and astronomy; and civil and military engines.

The first printed text was published in Rome around 1486, and the first illustrated edition in 1511. *De architectura* would become by far the most influential text on architecture ever written. Cynics sometimes suggest that Vitruvius' highly oblique style of writing is part of the appeal: subsequent architects could interpret him any way they wished. In any case, the future revered him. Throughout the antique revival of the Renaissance, the classical phase of the Baroque, and even in the Neoclassical period, Vitruvius' work was the chief authority on ancient classical architecture. A vast number of translations in nearly all European languages was published.

projects in their entirety. Marcus Agrippa, son-in-law to Augustus, built an entire aqueduct at his own expense, alleviating the problem of supplying Rome's population with a million cubic metres of water every day.

As can be imagined, providing adequate water supplies was only part of a complex system of urban administration. Rome had a fire service, consisting at one point of seven brigades manned by a thousand firemen. It also had a divisional system, just like a modern city, for effective local enforcement of law and order.

Gradually the fabric of Rome began to acquire greater formality until it was defined by a connecting network of great squares bordered by great buildings and statuary. Its wide streets featured many public activities and institutions including theatres and arenas. Public gatherings were fundamental to Rome's character, and there seems to have been an endless appetite for creating formal meeting places.

To the Forum Caesarum were added the Forum Augustum, the Forum of Vespasian, the Forum of the Emperor Nerva and the Forum of Trajan. Meanwhile, at a higher level, the City of Rome continued to act as a grand stage for a sequence of triumphal arches and gateways, each commemorating some new military victory.

form & reason

Architecture played a fundamental role in the development and shaping of the Roman Empire. In fact, in terms of influence, architecture takes its place alongside the other great durable achievement of the Romans: the legal codes (Lex Romana) upon which the laws of subsequent Western civilisations were based.

For Roman architecture was first and foremost symbolic, a testament to order, planning and the value of citizenship. As the Empire grew it also became an expression of the military genius and power. Roman architecture was a centuries-long programme of building design whose practicality and symbolism seemed indivisible. Even more than Greece, Rome embodied triumphalism combined with seemingly indomitable self-confidence. However, there was a sequence to these twin impulses. Before the Empire had come the republics and that was where the concept of sophisticated town planning began.

Pompeii: A Time Capsule

Pompeii, the ancient city of Campania in Italy would have been consigned to obscurity by history had it not been built near Mount Vesuvius. This was a location that proved fatally unlucky for its inhabitants of A.D. 79 but fortunate indeed for posterity. Pompeii was built on a spur formed by a prehistoric lava flow to the north of the mouth of the River Sarno and it was destroyed, together with neighbouring Herculaneum and Stabiae, by the violent eruption of Vesuvius whose lava entombed the three towns and in doing so gave future generations a unique time capsule view of Roman life.

Mount Vesuvius erupted on Aug. 24, AD 79. Volcanic debris buried Pompeii to a depth of nearly three metres. A rain of ashes followed, adding another three metres of detritus and – for the next 17 centuries – preserving the bodies of citizens and protecting the ruins from looting and climatic erosion.

When excavations began everyday objects were recovered intact. Murals and inscriptions were found, perfectly legible, on the walls of Pompeiian houses. The entire layout of the town could be identified. Two main streets enclosed by colonnades met in the town's main square. There was a forum complete with a council house, there were temples and basilicas. Just like innumerable cities since, Pompeii also had its small quarter of networked streets nestling between the main thoroughfares, in which shopkeepers and craftsmen carried out their daily trade. The value of Pompeii is inestimable. History often being a process of reconstruction, here for once was physical evidence of the ancient past of an almost miraculous sort.

above left An aerial view of the remarkable ruins of Pompeii, taken from an airship in 1913

above centre The Pompeii site with Mount Vesuvius in the distance

above right The Strada Abbondaza, one of the perfectly preserved main thoroughfares in Pompeii

The Roman town's strength lay in spatial composition. Borrowing freely from their Mediterranean predecessors the Romans created an architecture often derivative in detail but wholly original in its grand design. Monumental squares, wide streets with shops and offices, grand public spaces and complex drainage systems characterised what was clearly a major step forward in the development of intricate, organic cities.

If Greek and Hellenistic architecture had been largely based upon the contrast of vertical pillars with horizontal beams and lintels, the Romans parlayed those basics of architecture into a much more inventive and inclusive use of space. Despite many open spaces designed for public gatherings, Greek architecture had rarely been invitational in the sense that the public were expected to enter major buildings and become involved with internal spaces. As a result many Greek and Hellenistic architectural effects were designed primarily to please the eye or raise the spirit from their external aspect alone. The Romans, however, were enthusiastic interior designers, using walls and arches, domes and vaults, to create public buildings that strengthened the citizen's sense of involvement with the fabric – and by implication with the spirit – of the city. Roman architecture was to become almost as elaborate as the Empire it reflected, shaped by a rich variety of geographic, climatic, economic and social factors. Throughout the unifying element was the Roman predisposition for civic order, and it was achieved through a combination of intellectual rigour technological innovation and, most of all, cultural and practical borrowing.

technology & tradition

To today's eye, Roman architecture contained what seemed to be many contradictions. The fact that the Romans invented concrete seems to indicate that they were inclined towards experimentation and avant garde use of materials. Generally, though this was not the case. Like the Greeks before them, Roman architects were usually more concerned with the redeployment of familiar techniques and technologies, rather than experimenting with new ones.

The Romans are thought of as innovators, but they certainly borrowed heavily from the Greeks and other civilisations, often importing concepts wholesale – and with occasionally dubious logic. It is interesting to note that today's frequently criticised borrowings from architectural styles of the past – for example fake Tudor mansions and pastiche Regency façades with high-tech interiors – find clear parallels in Ancient Rome and indeed almost every period of history, even those which are popularly supposed to be somehow authentic in their antiquity.

Volcanic rock was the material most frequently used in the earliest Roman buildings . Known as tuff, this material came in varying hardnesses, some of it soft enough be sculpted. Eventually, other varieties of volcanic rock were used, usually harder, such as peperino and albani stone. As the Roman republic matured and the Empire grew, a limestone quarried mainly at Tivoli and known as travertine, came into widespread use. The exterior of the Colosseum in Rome uses travertine to good effect.

The Triumphal Arch

Often located at the entrance to a Forum, the Triumphal Arch is a defining Roman architectural element. As well as monuments, Triumphal Arches needed to be practical framing devices for victorious armies to march through with their large retinues of prisoners, and cart-laden booty, to the delight of cheering crowds.

In terms of design such arches often favoured the tall central arch flanked by two smaller ones, although sometimes a single arch sufficed. In either case the arches operated like ceremonial viaducts, supporting in this case not a thoroughfare but a massive architrave bearing the carved legend or dedication. The quality of lettering used offered a useful reminder to all those that followed down the centuries and which were indirectly influenced by Roman letters: clarity and legibility combined with elegance are the essence of any good typeface.

The Triumphal Arch has been likened to the image of a victorious legionnaire holding a banner on high, and to this day it is possible to see echoes of this most copied Roman building form in the image of triumphant sports fans holding pennants, scarves or banners aloft.

below The Triumphal Arch of the Emperor Tiberius, to be found in the town of Orange in France

Roman Doric

The Roman Doric order always had a base moulding. Examples can be seen in the Tabularium, Rome (78 B.C.) and on the Colosseum (A.D. 80).

Roman Ionic

The Ionic order was mainly used in temples and public buildings – notably the Temple of Fortuna Virilis and Trajan's Forum in Rome. Other remains suggest that the Ionic order may also have been used in some residential buildings.

Roman Corinthian

Most popular with the Romans was the richly decorative Corinthian order. When Roman general Sulla conquered Athens he removed from the Temple of Olympian Zeus columns which gave Rome the model to follow. Gradually the order became more highly detailed with dramatic high relief effects. Legend has it that inspiration for the Corinthian order came from the image of acanthus leaves entwined around a goblet, and whether or not this is true, it seems a suitable celebratory story for this most decorative style. Good examples exist at the temples of Mars Ultor and of Castor and Pollux in Rome.

above left A view of the Maison Carrée in Nimes, France, a fine example of Corinthian columns

At first marble was used mainly for decorative purposes. It could be set in cement and used as a rich facing material for humbler brick and concrete surfaces or for pavements in cut slabs or as mosaics.

Eventually though it became a much sought after material, rarer types being imported from all over the Empire along with porphyry, granite, and alabaster. The remains of the Flavian palace on the Palatine Hill in Rome still bear witness to this appetite for rare minerals.

The Romans were freed from the post-and-lintel structure that characterised (and limited) Greek architecture by their enthusiastic re-adoption of the arch.

As we have seen, the true arch went back as far as ancient Egypt, but the Romans used it with a flamboyant enthusiasm that was typical of their dynamic culture. In fact the Roman approach to most things could in many ways be likened to that of the United States of America in its founding period; the good ideas of other nations, which were as often as not undeveloped beyond the theoretical stage, were quickly adopted or adapted and put into vigorous production with the result that they developed quickly and profitably.

structures, shapes & forms

The Romans used columns and piers of brick, stone and occasionally concrete. They became supremely skilful at building a variety of arches which they introduced at the least opportunity into gates, bridges and aqueducts, as well as colonnades and doors.

Three main types of vault were favoured by the Romans: the barrel vault; the groined barrel vault; and the segmental vault. Here again facing was popular and the surfaces of Roman vaults were usually tiled or covered with stucco. The Basilica of Maxentius in Rome is a good example of this technique.

borrowed style

The Romans' most obvious borrowing from the Greeks was that of the Order. Changing their basic forms very little, the Romans appropriated the Greek orders and created from them five highly derivative orders of Roman architecture: Doric, Ionic, Corinthian, Tuscan, and Composite. Tuscan was a variant of the Greek Doric order, and Composite was based on the Greek Corinthian form.

The basic differences were that Roman columns were usually unfluted while the faces of the entablature, always left plain by the Greeks, became decorated, sometimes very elaborately. Increasingly the Romans were to develop a fondness for using the image of the classic Greek column rather than the substance.

Such columns were often fully or partially embedded into walls that were actually supported by other means entirely. A variant form of this was the pilaster, which was a shallow rectangular column which projected slightly beyond the wall into which it was built, and conformed to the order or style of the adjacent columns.

pont du gard, provence

The Arch

The true arch differs from the corbelled arch (where stones jutting from either side meet in opposition) in that is held together by pressure. Because the upper edge of any semi-circular array of stones has a greater circumference than the lower edge, each block must be cut as a wedge. These wedge-shaped stones are called voussoirs and their shape means that each presses firmly against the surface of its neighbour and so conducts the load uniformly. The central voussoir that holds the array in place is called the keystone. The point from which the arch rises from its vertical support is known as the spring.

One of the structural problems of the arc form is that its supports must be substantial enough to withstand the diagonal thrust delivered by the blocks and the loads they must bear. The arch will collapse if its supports are not either a) massive enough to buttress the thrust and conduct it into the foundations, or b) buttressed in some other way.

In most cases the Romans did not use mortar in their arches, relying instead on the precision of their stone cutting.

The arch is the essence of the viaduct, aqueduct and much else that defines Roman architecture.

the pantheon, rome

Concrete

The Romans developed the use of cast concrete mainly because, unlike the Greeks, they had limited access to local marble quarries. Roman concrete did not have the pouring qualities of the familiar contemporary product, but it did become a legitimate building material that could be laid in rough horizontal layers.

Roman concrete, opus caementicium, was a lime-based mortar containing volcanic sand and mixed with small aggregate. Its architectural significance was considerable. As well as being used for foundations it was also employed as an infill where it enabled Roman architects to construct more ambitious domes and vaults, leading to buildings that resembled a moulded shell rather than an assembly of planes. Roman concrete was never exposed, either internally or externally. A variety of facings – plaster, marble or decorative stone – disguised its essentially crude appearance.

left The Pantheon in Rome, which was built by the Emperor Hadrian between 120 and 124 A.D.

right The interior of the Pantheon's dome; with a huge diameter of over 43 metres, the combination of arches and concrete meant that pillars were not needed to support the structure

civic achievement

Public Purpose

For the modern city dweller Ancient Rome evokes many familiar issues and concerns. Alongside the grandeur and pomp of its monuments and the violence of its games and gladiatorial contests, Rome, like so many other urban centres, was on a day to day basis preoccupied with organising itself into a rational place. It sought to become a place in which the order of things was reflected in its physical layout, a city in which people would sense instinctively how to behave.

In Rome it was easy to distinguish between public spaces which were suited by their size and character for civic ceremonies, and those smaller spaces more appropriate to commerce and marketplaces. The city also featured reserved areas, not open to the public – palace courtyards and private areas and gardens. It also introduced a feature that architects and planners still experiment with today: the buffer zone that is neither inside nor out. The Roman colonnade, directly derived from its Greek antecedent, was exactly such a zone, enclosed and yet still not indoors, affording some protection from the elements but not isolated from the sound and movement of public activity in the forum.

The basilica became popular during the Roman Empire. Built of stone it was a spacious type of public hall in which legal and commercial business was conducted. Yet another example of how the Romans felt that any civic activity needed a building to match, the basilica offered the geometry of a central nave with (usually lower) side aisles, clerestory windows on both sides of the nave's upper walls, and a timber roof. Its form was later to be adopted by the Christian church and creates a link between Rome and the new religion of Christianity which was to be the engine of architectural development for the next 1000 years.

Domestic Facilities

Domus

The Romans were not the first to place great emphasis upon comfortable living. The Cretan preoccupation with comfort had been considerable. Running water passed beneath lavatories at the Palace of Knossos. Even the aqueduct predated Rome. The Romans, however, organised drainage for entire cities, not just select noblemen. Even so, social distinctions dictated who received what. In Roman society the rich lived in a house or domus which usually had individual lavatories, running water delivered from faucets, and the bathwater was heated in furnace-driven boilers. In the more temperate parts of the Roman Empire, heating took the form of portable coal-burning braziers. In colder climes and for public baths the floor was raised on brick pillars to allow slow furnaces below provide under-floor heating in a system known as hypocaust. Hot air from a hypocaust was channeled into a vertical flue in the wall of the room to be heated, through which hot air and smoke escaped into the open air. Where more warmth was needed, several flues would lead from the hypocaust, these flues consisting of hollow, oblong tiles set close together around the room. Many examples exist in house foundations across Europe.

Country Villas

The wealthy of Rome, like the wealthy of most wealthy cities today, kept a place in the country. Run by a hierarchy of staff in the master's absence, these were structures set in self-supporting grounds and usually took on secluded, sheltered geometries centered on atrium and courtyard. There was often a pluvium, (an area for collecting rainwater and providing a decorative pool), as well as gardens, fountains, covered walkways, plus an array of bedrooms, guestrooms, lavatories and other facilities for comfortable living.

Insulae

Working people lived in tenement blocks, such as the one whose ruins survive in Ostia Antica, Rome. Known as insulae, these early high-rise blocks had access to water from the street rather than a piped in supply. A single shared lavatory was situated on the ground floor. Proving again that certain human impulses are eternal, a commentator writing at the end of first century Rome noted how the landlord of dilapidated insulae were inclined to stave off imminent collapse with short term measures, including 'papering over cracks in ramshackle fabric'.

It is thought that insulae sometimes reached a height of six storeys and some had arcades of shops attached to them. The relatively poor sanitation was compensated for by the provision of, by today's standards, surprisingly luxurious public baths.

The Baths of Caracalla, for example, were so richly designed that they served as an aesthetic model for buildings throughout the ages, notably the now sadly demolished Pennsylvania Station in New York City, whose loss prompted a new awareness of architectural conservation in the United States in the 1960s.

The original Baths of Caracalla in Rome fared rather better, today being used as an opera house. In their original form they formed the centre of a complex of gardens and incorporated gymnasia and a building subdivided into hot room, medium-hot room and an open-air swimming pool.

above left The Via Di Diana, one of the roads through the ruined apartment blocks at Ostia Antica

above right A well-preserved example of an insulae dwelling place in the same street

46

caracalla

left The mosaic pavements in the Baths at Caracalla in Rome, with (above) a detail of the intricate design

the colosseum

above The most magnificent sports stadium of its day, the Colosseum as it now appears, a most familiar sight but still awesome in its sheer scale

architectural handbook on the Greek orders. The ground floor is Doric, the second floor Ionic and the third Corinthian. Pilasters run along the top storey, and so, ostensibly, we have a commemorative gâteau of Greek structural devices holding up Rome's greatest public monument. However closer inspection proves that the whole complex tracery of external orders is no more than icing on a quite different cake. The Greek orders here play no structural role at all – the columns are simply decorative devices – and the building is supported on invisible, built-in members.

Inside, the Colosseum is revealed as a truly vast auditorium capable of seating over 80,000 spectators. For once a state of ruin helps rather than hinders our appreciation of an original building, since the absence of the arena floor affords a view into the building's complex web of chambers and circulation passageways that would originally have been invisible. Cages, cells and restraining areas for animals and combatants were created by sealing off sections of passageway with portcullises, whilst mechanical and hydraulic lifts were used to raise them to the level of the arena floor. This is an elaborate subterranean world, entirely Roman in its fondness for organised effects and facilities and far removed from the simplicity of the original Greek model.

Above floor level the Colosseum's seating design addresses precisely the same concerns as the most modern stadium must. Its four tiers of seats are divided into segments separated by vaulted passages mathematically calculated to provide optimum speed of exit in case of fire.

The Colosseum was officially dedicated in A.D. 80 by Titus in a ceremony that included 100 days of games. Only later, in A.D. 82, did Domitian complete the building by adding the uppermost pilastered storey. The structure was damaged by lightning and earthquakes in medieval times and, even more severely, by vandalism through the centuries. Today all the original marble seats and decorative materials have disappeared.

The Colosseum

The Colosseum was a giant amphitheatre built in Rome under the Flavian emperors and originally called the Flavian Amphitheatre. Unlike earlier amphitheatres, which were nearly all embedded into hillsides for extra support, the Colosseum is a freestanding structure of stone and concrete, measuring 188 by 155 metres. Like so much Roman architecture it is derived from a Greek model, although the Colosseum is particularly interesting because it is so definitively Roman in character. Greek theatres were used exclusively for drama – intellectual games, if you like. The Colosseum, though, was used for real and bloody games, since most of its dramas took the form of violent fights between men and animals, gladiators and slaves as well as elaborate stagings of larger combats, including mock naval engagements.

The Colosseum, elliptical in shape, stands in the centre of Rome, and even today, stripped of many of its trappings and long deserted by gladiatorial activity, manages to be a magnificent piece of architectural theatre all by itself. Everything about the building underlines the importance Rome placed upon great public gatherings, complex organisation and grand monumentality.

Construction of the Colosseum began sometime between A.D. 70 and 72 and it was completed in A.D. 82. The drama begins on the outside, very Greek flavoured with its four storey façade acting almost as an

Decline & Fall

Rome reached the peak of its grandeur and ancient population (estimated at more than 1 million) during the late 1st and early 2nd centuries. At this point its population probably began to decline; at the height of an outbreak of the plague in the reign of Marcus Aurelius, 2000 people a day died.

By the 3rd century economic and political bad fortune added to Rome's slow decline. As ever, life was reflected in building so that when Aurelian built walls around Rome, they were more an expression of concern about possible barbarian attack than triumphal expression of Rome's power. Rome's command of refined urban technology was by now applied only haphazardly to the city's social problems, and many of the citizens were forced to live in overcrowded slum conditions. The anticipated barbarian invasions of Italy during the 5th century were massive and further hastened Rome's decline. The founding of Constantinople confirmed Rome's loss of political supremacy and despite the Emperor Constantine's restoration of many of the buildings and monuments of imperial Rome, its day as the heart of an empire was finished. Furthermore, Constantine's support of Rome's small Christian community laid the foundations of the city's Christian and papal future.

4

from early christian

forms to islam

above The interior of the eight-sided Basilica of Saint Simeon at Qalaat Semaan in Northern Syria

early christian

Christianity gave rise to no churches of any description and indeed very few buildings at all during its early stages. This was partly due to the fact that its first adherents were a poverty-stricken and persecuted minority, and partly because first-wave Christianity was anyway rooted in simple communal living and expectation of a second coming, not in ceremony, shrines or buildings of worship.

It would take 200 years for Christianity to become accepted to the point where the lineaments of the Roman Empire might be used as a conduit for spreading the word and longer still before the trappings of a new architecture begin to emerge.

When the first Christian emperor of the Roman Empire Constantine I finally declared Christianity the official religion in A.D. 313, a new era began in which, very gradually and with scant clear-cut stylistic developments, the old culture of Rome and the new forms of Christianity began to blend and intermingle. It was a process of adaptive use rather than of new architectural inspiration. Eventually, though, a single defining form emerged. The basilica more than any other building form lent itself to the newly authorized religion of Christianity. Although at first used for little more than communal accommodation, the basilica was to prove itself a particularly appropriate form to develop in concert with the architectural needs of the Christian faith.

Constantinople

When in A.D. 330 Constantine, in an attempt to strengthen the increasingly dissolute Roman empire, refounded Byzantium as Constantinople, the opportunity arose to build a brand new city there. Constantine's new metropolis would become one of the great world capitals, a city of enormous wealth and beauty and, in ambition at least, Rome reborn. The new capital certainly repositioned the power centre of the Roman Empire, moving it to the east, with what were to be far-reaching cultural and architectural implications. These included a rich blending of the built forms of East and West, a process that was conditioned and shaped by a blend of Christian religion, Roman organisation, and inherited Greek temperament.

Constantine established new city walls that more than doubled the size of Byzantium, which now contained imperial buildings, a huge palace, administrative halls, major churches, and streets decorated with statues plundered from rival cities. In an imaginative inducement to expand the city rapidly, free bread and citizenship were bestowed on those willing to move inside the newly expanded city limits.

This calculated reinvention of Byzantium also promoted a widespread church building programme throughout the empire. Almost without exception these churches, from Rome to Bethlehem, took the basilican form and adapted it to what would be the model for all Western churches of the next 900 years.

Salonica & Ravenna

Despite the immense contemporary importance of Constantinople, virtually nothing remains of its architecture today. Only the ruins of the church of St John Studios still exist, revealing a colonnaded nave and semicircular apse.

Salonica in northern Greece has more surviving churches from the 5th century A.D., including that of St. Demetrios which has a nave whose arcades feature unusually intricate groupings of columns and piers within a strikingly composed architectural space.

Ravenna, in Northern Italy contains some of the finest Early Christian churches which were increasingly becoming richer and more complex. Here the church of S. Croce built by the Empress Galla Placidia in A.D. 420 boasted the addition of a cross-shaped mausoleum decorated with luminous mosaics that recall the elegant spirit of Hellenism.

The End of The Empire

Soon the spirit of the age would turn to the more complex spirit of Byzantine art and architecture. Early Christian architecture – and the ethos of the ancient world in general – came to an end with the final fall of the Roman Empire in A.D. 476, a process so fragmentary that ironically – given its record of apparently unstoppable vigour, scope and achievement – occurred almost imperceptibly.

the beginnings of islam

Three hundred years after Early Christian architecture began to evolve into the rich patterns of the Byzantine style there began a new religion which was to make an enormous impact upon the West's perception of the built environment, despite the fact that its roots were in the East and its excursions into Europe proper were limited mainly to Spain.

Islam started with the teachings of Prophet Muhammad in Arabia in the 7th century A.D. The term islam, means literally 'surrender,' and so neatly encapsulates a fundamental precept of Islam, namely that its adherents, Muslims, surrender to the will of Allah which is revealed in the holy text of the Quran.

Islam, as taught by Muhammad to a small band of disciples, spread rapidly through the Middle East to Africa, Europe, the Indian subcontinent, the Malay Peninsula and China. One of the religion's defining characteristics is its sense of community, something which differed significantly from the Romans' sense of empire and state but which in fact echoed the roots of Christianity. This communal characteristic was also eventually to resurface the layout of Islamic towns and cities.

The roots of Islamic architecture are, however, exceptionally difficult to determine. Any architecture that grows out of a tent-dwelling nomadic culture clearly has an individual approach that distinguishes it from that of most other cultures. For example, the Bedouins who carried out the first Islamic conquests in Syria, Persia and Palestine, subjugated their newly acquired cities and then, instead of building monuments to their faith, simply set about modifying existing buildings for that purpose. Christian churches that had once been temples now became mosques. Lacking any experience of building permanent structures and having had no need of them until their religion decreed it, the Bedouins simply changed what was already there to correspond to the immediate requirements of their own faith. This sometimes involved nothing more than simple conversion, but occasionally an existing Christian church would become incorporated into a larger religious complex.

The process found one of its earliest expressions in the Umayyad Mosque, also known as the Great Mosque, built in Damascus between A.D. 705 and 715 by the Umayyad Caliph al-Walid I. This is certainly the earliest surviving stone mosque, and it originally incorporated both pagan fragments – a 1st-century Hellenic temple to Jupiter – and elements of a later Christian church. There is even a shrine to a relic honoured by both Muslims and Christians: the head of St. John the Baptist.

With a large rectangular plan of 156 by 100 metres, the mosque contains an open courtyard surrounded by an arcade of columned arches. A hall of worship, running the length of the south side of the structure, is divided into three long aisles by more columns and arches. A transept with a central octagonal dome bisects the aisles centrally. Here too is evidence of one of the style's most enduring and recognisable features: the geometric interlaced pattern, a synthesis of the decorative and the formal that has come to symbolise Islamic architecture. The Umayyad Mosque's south wall windows' marble grilles are wrought in this interlaced pattern.

The mosque's walls were originally covered with vast swathes of mosaics depicting an idealized landscape which probably represented the Quran's image of paradise. Today only a few fragments of the mosaics have survived and the Great Mosque itself suffered much damage in the 15th century and a fire at the end of the 19th century. Although a shadow of its former self, The Umayyad Mosque nonetheless remains both a major architectural monument and a prefiguring symbol of how Islamic architecture would establish itself in the near East and parts of Europe through a process of infiltration and adaptation.

three great mosques

During the rule of the Umayyad prince al-Walid I (705-715), a number of complex developments within the Muslim community were reflected in the creation of three major mosques. These mosques were built at Medina, Jerusalem, and Damascus. Even the locations themselves were revealing. Medina was the city in which the Muslim state was formed and in which its Prophet was buried. Jerusalem was a symbolic place to Jews, Christians, and Muslims. Damascus, meanwhile, was a historic city most recently revered as the capital of the new Islamic empire.

These mosques were imperial buildings created to symbolize the importance of the Islamic state as well as the permanence of Islam and its parity with other faiths. The age-old architectural trick of galvanizing abstract aspirations by means of building monuments to them had once again been worked. These mosques were considerably more than traditional places to pray.

Although the plans of al-Aqsa Mosque in Jerusalem – and those of the one at Medina – can be reconstructed with a fair degree of certainty, only

Mosques

A mosque is technically any house or space dedicated to prayer in Islam. The 'collective mosque' – which is what popular non-Islam imagination usually conjures when hearing the word – is the centre of community worship. In the early days of the Islam religion, the collective mosque doubled as the venue for several public functions and in later centuries often included courthouses, schools and libraries.

The earliest mosques took as their model a form of domestic architecture since their inspiration was the courtyard of the Prophet Muhammed's house at Medina where he used to pray.

Subsequently mosques underwent various shifts of architectural style, frequently responding to strictly local conditions, but usually retaining a large area, sometimes open, sometimes roofed, with a minaret nearby or attached. Initially any convenient raised place, the minaret eventually became the tower that the word now connotes and is used as an equivalent to the Christian church tower bell.

A strict geometry dominates within, with a curved niche for the leader of prayers facing Mecca, and adjacent steps leading to a pulpit. The floor is covered with carpets although statues and other likenesses are strictly forbidden.

below A detail of the mosaic from the Great Mosque – the Umayyad Mosque – at Damascus, which was built between 705 and 715 A.D.

right The courtyard of the Great Mosque, which is the earliest mosque to have survived intact

The Medina Mosque

The Medina mosque was essentially a large hypostyle with a courtyard. A hypostyle is an interior space where the roof rests on massive pillars or columns avoiding the need for arches. The necessary bulk and number of supports – ostensibly a drawback, since they took up a lot of space and could be visually very ponderous – could be turned to advantage when the columns were used for carving motifs.

The colonnades at Medina were of varying depth on all four sides.

Al-Aqsa Mosque

History suggests that the Al-Aqsa Mosque, a former Jewish temple, consisted of many naves, perhaps over a dozen, sited parallel to one other in a north-south direction. There was no courtyard because the huge esplanade of the former temple could be used as an open space in front of the building.

The Umayyad Mosque

The Umayyad Mosque of Damascus was also an adaptive building: its outer limits and three gates were parts of a Roman temple forming a rectangle 156 by 100 metres.

The interior consists of an open space surrounded on three sides by a portico and of a covered space of three equal long naves cut in the middle by a perpendicular nave.

The Minaret

Minaret is the Arabic word for beacon and the form it describes is one of the defining features of Islamic religious architecture. It is the tower or towers (the number of minarets to each mosque can vary from one to six) from which the faithful are called to prayer five times each day by a *muezzin*, or crier. A minaret is always connected to a mosque and has one or more balconies or open galleries. The minaret is almost certainly another example of how human patterns of behaviour, at first informal and opportunistic can become codified and finally symbolized by structures. At the time of the Prophet Muhammad, the call to prayer was made from any handy high spot near the mosque. How much more potent to have a distinctively-shaped bespoke tower as part of the ritual.

The first minarets were part of Islam's adaptive phase, being old Greek watchtowers or the towers of Christian churches. The oldest minaret in North Africa is at al-Qayrawan, Tunisia and was built between A.D. 724 and 727.

Minarets are constructed in a wide variety of forms ranging from thick, squat spiral ramps, as at Samarra, Iraq (built A.D. 848-852), to soaring, slim spires. Frequently a minaret has a square base where it joins the mosque but above it can develop into a series of circular, hexagonal, or octagonal stages, each with its projecting balcony. At the top is the distinctive dome or an open pavilion reached by internal or external steps.

The upper parts of a minaret is often richly decorated with elaborate carving. From practical platform to a universally recognized symbol, minarets were developed to be the landmarks of Islam.

right An example of the intricate marble tilework to be found in the window grilles of the Great Mosque

the mosque at Damascus has been preserved with comparatively minor alterations and repairs. In general outline the three buildings appear at first glance to be quite different from each other.

All three mosques incorporated a number of new practical elements and boldly symbolic meanings. A feature known as a *mihrab*, for example, appears in all mosques. This is a niche of varying size that is usually heavily decorated and its purpose was to commemorate the symbolic presence of the Prophet. Only the Damascus mosque deployed an existing feature – the old towers of the Roman building – as minarets to call the faithful to prayer and visually advertise the presence of Islam in a non-Muslim geographical context.

All three mosques had an axial nave, a feature that served both the design and various ceremonial purposes when a prince's retinue needed to be accommodated.

Finally, all three buildings were heavily decorated with marble, mosaics, and woodwork and there is enough evidence to suggest that all three placed great emphasis upon formal composition and visual balance. When compared to the earliest adaptive Muslim buildings of, the great mosques of al-Walid were quite complex in form, extremely well built and had by now acquired some uniquely features.

Although the external appearance and proportions were individually determined by unique local conditions, the internal balance between open and covered areas and the multiplicity of supports indicate the strength of the early hypostyle form.

secular style

Obviously the religious buildings of early Islam took the forms they did in response to the faith. However, secular Muslim architecture had no particularly Islamic character in terms of building forms and features. In general little was destroyed by conquering Muslim armies and therefore there was no immediate need to rebuild or, for that matter, to reshape, existing commercial, residential and manufacturing areas. Much early Islamic secular architecture resembles that of many regions, even those of the West. Gradually though, even the most adaptive of cultures, which Islam was, feels the need to impose its own cultural values, and this it did in the development of Umayyad and early 'Abbasid secular architecture.

Palaces

As the Muslim princes in Syria and Iraq became rich in money and resources they began to establish a new palace architecture. The relationship of the palace to the city is very well illustrated the construction of Baghdad between 762 and 766-767 A.D. by the 'Abbasid caliph al-Mansur. Baghdad was a circular walled city supposedly symbolic of the navel of the universe. It was entered through a spectacular series of gates each leading to an axial commercial street which served to separate the segments of a dense ring of residential quarters. In the centre of the city was situated a large open space containing a palace, a mosque, and a handful of administrative buildings. It should be stressed that this

structured approach to an urban centre was driven more by Baghdad's role as a walled palace than its status as a city. Whilst it clearly was a city by all acceptable definitions, such a calculated spatial arrangement rarely existed where no palace was to be found.

We should not forget that the Muslim empire became a vast region extending from the Mediterranean to India, and now, for the first time since the days of Alexander the Great, a diverse series of regions became culturally unified. As a result, previously diffused design and architectural styles became available in single locations leading to a potentially rich synthesis of styles.

Urbanization

Equally importantly, the wealth of the new princes gave a fresh impetus to urban life and to trade. New cities sprang up from the edge of the Moroccan Sahara to northeastern Iran, and by the 9th century A.D. Arab merchants were trading in regions as remote as China.

As a result, urbanization was one of the most characteristic features of early Muslim civilization.

Unlike Roman towns, Islamic urban centres had no master planning. Even palaces and mosques (where they occurred in a town at all) whose Roman equivalents would have been precisely-calculated markers in a structured urban gird, were often located quite arbitrarily and even oddly. However, great organizational effort was lavished on water distribution and conservation, and there are some 9th century A.D. cisterns to be seen in Tunisia, a device designed to measure the Nile's level in Cairo. and a series of complex elaborate dams, canals, and sluices at Qasr al-Hayr in Syria.

Such features aside however, Islamic societies were perhaps most notable for the way in which the traditional grid format of the Roman

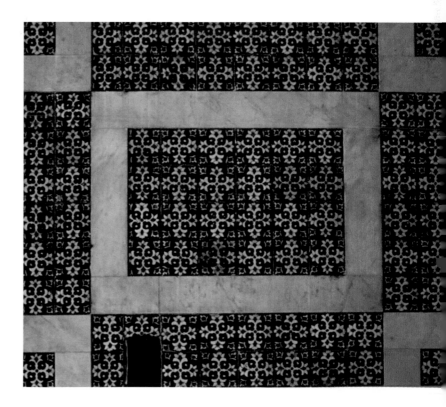

colonies gradually gave way to new geometries which were more in sympathy with the patterns of Islamic life.

Typically a Roman-style town would be laid out in bold rectilinear blocks punctuated with clearly defined civic features like open-air markets and theatres. The same town embraced by a later Islamic culture – Damascus, perhaps, or Mérida – would take on, over a period of time, the delineations of a very different society. As soon as the public places of Roman society became irrelevant to the new citizenry, they were nothing more than obstacles to be eroded by fresh footpaths that would gradually transform the original grid into an organic network of private communications. Furthermore, the Roman tendency to house families in discrete accommodation arranged in city block format – either as separate units or in multi-storey apartment buildings – became a plan irrelevant to the Islamic societies that followed. There, a non-centralized approach to urban living meant a far more organic arrangement of tribes, clans and families for whom the remains of the main through streets acted as barriers and segregators as much as common conduits.

Organic Town Planning

There is good reason to believe that these cultural attributes, despite the very temporary fabric of city street and domestic house (which of course would never last through the centuries anything like as well as major churches or imperial buildings), were nonetheless enduring and robustly exportable. Old Delhi and Marrakech have remarkably similar characteristics that find fragmentary echoes in Spain and other parts of Europe where Islam made its mark.

What were the cultural sources of this non-celebratory building and town planning? As we have seen, where no palace existed to absorb the identity of a town, the overriding factor of Islamic urban centres was that no grand plan was imposed and its cities tended to take on the shape prescribed by custom, ownership and the Islamic requirement for visual privacy. This last requirement, for example might determine where doors and windows would be positioned on a building or how high the building would rise. Neither would one of Western architecture's favourite devices, the visual corridor – a formalized invitation to gaze – be encouraged or allowed. Houses themselves would be designed from the inside out, internal arrangements or spatial with neighbours across a courtyard receiving far more thought than the external appearance of the street-side front of the house.

As the old geometries of grand public spaces became eroded, Islamic buildings would creep across them, often bridging squares and streets, interlocking with other buildings and generally establishing an organic, improvisational style that precluded 'fresh-start' town planning.

Formal town planning rules did exist, although they too were of an engagingly simple and practical nature: the minimum street width may have been decreed in the Quran by the Prophet, but it was still that which would allow a fully-laden camel to pass through it. Planting trees in a public right of way was not permitted, cul-de-sacs were commonly owned by all whose property fronted onto them.

The enduring quality of such organic and apparently disordered urban forms was that whilst they might seem chaotic to the outsider, they contained a perfectly acceptable logic of their own. They were not ramshackle in the sense of a neat civic order that had gone to rack and ruin, rather they were the expression of a fundamentally different set of rules, in this case rules generated by a society that defined itself on an individual basis rather than in accordance with some imposed centralized rulebook like that of Rome.

This original organic quality of Islamic towns is something of which, unfortunately, little material evidence endures. For this reason alone its legacy tends to be overshadowed by that of Islam's complex religious architecture, where the often stunning effects of bright sunlight falling on sharply-cut patterns remains one of its architecture's most potent and spectacular characteristics.

Even so, the natural and organic approach of the Islamic urban centre demonstrated its ability not only to exist at home, but to survive and be accomodated in far-flung lands abroad too.

Building Technology

As with building styles, Islamic architecture was more of a borrower than an innovator, using local materials in much the same way as they had always been used before. Therefore stone and brick were favoured in the Mediterranean countries, while plaster-covered mud brick was used in the Middle East, in Iran and Iraq.

The most important innovation took place in Iraq, where a style of architecture based on baked brick was developed during the 9th century. It was a technique which was to be subsequently utilized inbuilding in both Syria and Egypt.

In early Islamic architecture roofs were usually supported by the walls which were usually undecorated and often buttressed with half towers. When columns and capitals were used these were either adaptations from pre-Islamic buildings or direct imitations of older forms.

Columns might be covered with arches although these were not used in any rational structural way – i.e. to reduce the bulk of the supports – but rather as a feature for their own sake. This led to the development of multi-pointed arches, complex, multi-centred variants of the round arch which, with its semi-circular form, is single-centred.

The Great Mosque at Córdoba had two rows of superimposed horseshoe arches of alternating stone and brick apparently deployed to break up the monotony of a hypostyle building, where the roof is held up by massive and numerous columns.

Most early Islamic ceilings were flat-roofed although gabled wooden roofs appear in the Muslim world west of the Euphrates.

The dome was used in a variety of building types – mosques, mausoleums, and secular buildings.

right A contemporary mosque, showing the adaptation of traditional elements, in Regent's Park, London

from early christian forms to islam

islam in spain

In the second half of the 7th century A.D. there was a Muslim invasion of Spain, the result of both expansionism and a response by a Muslim leader called Tariq to call for assistance from a dispossessed leader in the ancient Roman province of Baetica, now Andalusia (the name Al-Andalus was conferred the Muslim invaders). A Muslim army led by Tariq duly sailed across the Strait of Gibraltar in A.D. 711, triumphed in a decisive battle and instead of returning to Africa, marched north to conquer the Visigothic capital of Toledo. Soon more Islam forces joined the invasion and subsequently captured Mérida, Saragossa and, eventually, Seville .

Seville

An inland port, it is today the chief city of Andalusia and the fourth largest in Spain. It became a capital of Muslim Spain having previously flourished under Roman rule as Hispalis, the administrative centre of the province of Baetica. When it fell to the Muslims, Seville flourished once again, enjoying great prosperity and ambitious building programmes until Muslim possession ended in 1248 when Moorish and Jewish minorities were driven into exile, and the local economy collapsed.

The oldest part of Seville lies on the left bank of the Guadalquivir and today still reflects its Islamic past in a complex a maze of narrow and twisting streets, tightly enclosed squares, and Moorish style houses. The patterns of living and trade that go on in this quarter of the town today – self regulating informality and informal co-operation – still echo the Islamic civic model that originated on another continent 1500 years ago.

Although the legacy of Islam can be seen persisting right through the Middle Ages in Cefalù, Sicily and in Palermo's Royal Palace, in direct terms Islamic architecture penetrated Europe in only a very limited way. The advances into Spain and even central France left an extraordinary local legacy, but it could be argued that as a force for defining the city Islam remains outside the European traditions and too fragmented to be of great importance. This may be true, and yet the Islamic approach to the built environment somehow remains a compelling model, perhaps more so today in a world of instant communications and cultural cross-reference than ever before. The lessons of Islam for *laissez-faire* town planning still provide a proven basis for letting the local population define its own environment through local experience rather than central prescription.

On a more formal level Islamic architecture had an extraordinary potential. The fact that figurative representation was forbidden concentrated invention in the field of largely abstract forms – a restriction that resulted in a kind of freedom of invention. For example the arcades of the mosque originally required only light supports for their awnings, so freeing designers to create a multiplicity of decorative arch-shapes that would later be translated into complex structural forms as at The Great Mosque at Córdoba. Also in Islam calligraphic flourishes were translated into three-dimensional structures with great flair. As a balance of freedom and restraint, license and control, Islamic architecture is a fascinating synthesis of the spiritual force and social values that prompted it.

left A view from a covered pavilion into one of the tranquil gardens of the Alhambra Palace in Granada

below The fabulous interior of the dome at the Alcazar Palace in Seville

The Alhambra, Granada

Built between 1309 and 1354 The Alhambra Palace complex in Granada, Spain, is an opulent example of what Islamic palace architecture could achieve. The Alhambra's hill site had been occupied by citadels and other fortified buildings for three centuries before two successive princes, Yusuf I and Muhammad V, transformed it into a residence of staggering magnificence. Today little remains of that magnificence. There are several gates built in the form of triumphal arches, and the remains of some forecourts, but only three sections remain intact. Of the section of the Alhambra built by Yusuf I, the long Court of the Myrtles has survived, leading to the vast Hall of Ambassadors in one of the outside towers.

There is also the Court of the Lions, with its decorative stalactites (muqurnas) and its famous lion fountain at the centre, giving on to numerous other rooms including the intricately decorated Hall of the Abencerrajes and the Hall of the Two Sisters. The third section, predating the first two, is a summer residence built higher up the hill in surrounding gardens full of fountains, pavilions, and covered walkways.

The remains of the Alhambra are particularly significant to architectural historians, not only because it is one of the few palaces to have survived from medieval Islamic times in any substantial form at all, but because it provides excellent examples of a number of architectural concerns otherwise known to us only through writings. For example it perfectly exemplifies that same inward-looking quality that can be found in the most humble Muslim residence: the calculated contrast between modest exterior and private interior. Here of course the private interior is a highly-decorated exercise in architectural brilliance, but the principle holds.

Here too can be seen the Islamic reverence of water, in its ubiquitous presence as baths, as static basins of water, or as a moving feature as a fountain. Also we can see the apparent lack of overall plan so indicative of Islamic building, various elements simply attached to each other.

The Alhambra was mainly decorated in stucco, much of it flat, but occasionally leaping into rich relief, like the highly complex *muqurnas* of the cupolas in the Hall of the Two Sisters. This preponderance of high-level decoration creates a strange effect with heavy, richly-ornamented ceilings supported by thin columns or lace-like walls penetrated by many windows. As with so much of Islam, there is an apparent rejoicing in contradiction, and irony with individual elements fused in a symbolic *tour de force*.

above   A long shot of the Alhambra showing the Palace's full extent

below   A detail of the stucco carvings at the Alhambra

right   The pillored open pavilions that open out into the numerous gardens of the Alhambra

far right   The detailed filigree carvings surrounding a typical Alhambra Palace window

Cologne Cathedral

medieval europe

medieval europe

5

age of darkness

From the year 500 the remains of the Western Roman Empire began to disintegrate into a complex patchwork of tribal and regional states. What was left of Classical civilization collapsed under a wave of fragmented local customs, laws and tribal rules. Trade ground to a halt all along the Mediterranean, depressing economies and, in the process, effectively eradicating urban life. Cities no longer existed, at least in no way that would have been recognisable to Greece or Rome.

Even Rome itself, once a million-strong city, withered in this new dark age to numbers that would only half fill the average modern sports stadium. All that was left were ragged settlements barely qualifying for the name village, and the male population of Europe consisted mainly of peasants, priests and soldiers. Little was built and most of the old building skills were lost.

Our investigation of The City's progress comes to a halt, or at least a long hiatus, until the 11th century when primitive towns began to reform. Even the poorer citizens of ancient Rome had enjoyed far more sophisticated living conditions than almost anyone in early medieval Europe. Today, when instant global communications mean that information distribution is cumulative and progressive, it seems unthinkable to us that yesterday's knowledge could ever actually become lost and yesterday's progress undone.

That, though, is what happened in the Middle Ages when even those clues to the past that did exist were often less accessible to those living at the time than they are to us today. However two historical forces did persist, offering at least the possibility of reclaiming something of the values of the lost civilizations. One was largely abstract – the ancient ideal of Rome and its Empire, which still subsisted in the minds of many ambitious leaders. The other was Rome's architecture. Roman architecture in general, and the early monuments of Christianity in particular, had endured well enough to offer a tangible link with an otherwise lost past. This twin capability of architecture to suggest immortality and to enshrine aesthetic values made it a singularly effective focus for anyone wishing to promote their own kingdom to the scale of an empire. Comes the moment, comes the man.

In 800 A.D. Charlemagne, having struck one of history's more inspired deals, was crowned Holy Roman Emperor by Pope Leo III in Rome. Charlemagne's burgeoning empire was more a political assemblage of Western Europe's fragments – albeit now endorsed by the papacy – than anything to rival the Roman model. Even so it provided a galvanizing and unifying force that was to prove immensely successful. With a papal sponsor for spiritual credibility, the surviving buildings of Christianity to act as venerable markers, and Rome's language and literature to act as cultural media for a renaissance of classical values, Charlemagne – Carolus Magnus in Latin – initiated a revival that would come to be known as Carolingian Romanesque.

carolingian romanesque

In truth the buildings that emerged under the influence of Charlemagne and his contemporaries were of very mixed pedigree, some being very conservative copies of classical Roman buildings, others being strange re-interpretations that incorporated a mish-mash of barbarian styles, and still others that made a brave attempt to look to the future. Even so, there was a unifying spirit about them if not a consistent aesthetic, and in the context of history these 'Roman-esque' aspirations look sufficiently legitimate to warrant their historical title.

The Palatine Chapel was Charlemagne's imperial chapel (it now forms part of the Cathedral of Aachen, Germany), and was part of a complex of buildings that acted as both royal court and national church. The Palatine Chapel was designed by Odo of Metz, who based it on the Church of San Vitale at Ravenna, modifying the original's late antique origins with characteristics of classic Roman architecture that evoked something of the theatrical feel of The Colosseum.

Representative of the more eclectic type of Carolingian church was that of Germigny-des-Prés, near Orléans, France, which was based on a Byzantine model but had all its apses formed in the horseshoe shape favoured by Islamic designers. This Islamic touch is probably due to the origins of its founder, the Bishop of Orléans whom Charlemagne had brought from Spain. Although it is the sole survivor of Islamic influence in early Romanesque buildings, it was in all probability only one of several such hybrid forms.

above The gateway to the monastery at Lorsch, Germany, built around 800 A.D.

left Charlemagne's Palatine Chapel at Aachen, Germany, designed by Odo of Metz and built 788 to 805 A.D.

return to darkness

The death of Charlemagne in 814 A.D. demonstrated that the revival he inspired and partially implemented had been insecurely based on his own popularity. Cultural decline, political chaos and invasion from all points of the compass reduced Europe to a shambles for another 100 years. Gradually though stability returned, with the various invading forces settling in different parts of the continent and, on becoming assimilated, slowly re-establishing some degree of stability. Economic conditions began to improve and urban life, with its craftsmen and artisans, slowly returned. This improvement was strictly comparative.

Domestic housing was still often rudimentary timber shacks, cities hardly existed in the ancient sense at all and much of Europe was still highly dangerous and unstable. With relative prosperity came the start of a new cultural revival however, this time one that was heavily biased towards religious fervour. This fervour expressed itself in many ways, none more significant than a widespread tendency for mass pilgrimages to obscure destinations. This susceptibility found its logical conclusion in The Crusades, an early historical example of one culture's usually ill-advised and always very expensive military forays into distant foreign territory; in this case it was to The Holy Land to reclaim what was considered 'Christian' territory from the Muslims.

This new culture founded upon spiritual enthusiasm and regained prosperity resulted, unsurprisingly, in many new churches being built all over Europe. They did not all enjoy a uniform style, nor did they all spring up simultaneously – Europe was still a dislocated patchwork of power bases even in times of relative uniformity of spirit. However the spirit of this particular age was once again one of hope – hope of re-building the present along the lines of the perceived past. The building styles that expressed that hope became collectively known as Romanesque.

romanesque

Romanesque is no more than a label given to a collection of linked architectural styles that developed in Europe in the mid-11th century. These styles did not have a label at all until 1818, when Romanesque was coined by Charles-Alexis-Adrien de Gerville, for whom it suggested nothing more than a Roman-like quality. This Roman-like quality varied considerably from region to region, and despite its complex provenance the Romanesque style had at least one unifying building type, a result of the spirit of religious reawakening that had prompted it in the first place: the monastery. From around 650 to 1200 A.D. a movement to found monasteries, begun by Charlemagne, had resulted in a series of buildings that at the same time symbolised the Christian Life and offered sanctuary in what was still a violent and quarrelsome continent.

Monasteries

Communication and transport by whatever means was difficult and hazardous, with the result that numerous self-sufficient neighbourhoods developed. In these circumstances, any large monastery tended to take over – or at least duplicate – the role of city, offering its immediate surrounding areas a selection of administrative, spiritual and practical amenities. Occasionally monasteries existed on the edge of larger towns, close to the walls. Even then, as likely as not it was the monasteries that were the engines of invention and progress. The Cistercian order, for example, was responsible for all the agricultural innovations of the time, notably in land drainage, sheep-rearing and dry stone walling. As conditions improved generally, monastic buildings and their surrounding structures became better organised, better constructed, and generally more authoritative. Their own improvements as well as their encouragement of re-establishing the practice of trades and professions – stonemasonry, carving, engineering and joinery – prepared the ground for better religious and domestic architecture. In short, the church had taken over some of the functions of the state.

Even so, in places it was left to other forces to impose some sort of order. In the Western Empire that force was the feudal system developed by the Normans. As a system it was a crude one, but it was nonetheless a system, something which Europe had now lacked for centuries. The clergy remained the only literate members of society. Labourers lived in huts of wattle-and-daub (basket-woven wood strips covered with mud, dung and horsehair and covered with rudimentary plaster). Their lords lived in halls that prefigured the manor house or castle, large single rooms with a central hearth and a crude smoke hole above .

above the Benedictine Abbey of Sainte Foy, built between 1035 and 1060, at Conques, France

far left The cloisters in the Church of Saint Martin at Tours, France

below left The Church of St. Lawrence, Bradford-on-Avon, England

Vaulting

One of Romanesque's unifying forces came in a response to the high fire risks ever present in predominantly timber environments. The Romans had never succeeded in creating a fireproof basilican church, but by 1000 A.D. the monastic builders had begun to solve this problem through the use of vaulting. Gradually various vaulting systems developed as the solution to large span building. Tunnel vaults were favoured in France and Spain, groin vaults in Germany, domes in the south-western region of France, rib vaults in parts of England and Italy. The characteristic of Romanesque church building is its semi-circular shape, the same shape as the round arch and barrel vault which can be traced back to Rome. Latterly the structure of churches became more expressive than their classical models, with brick arches and vaults exposed rather than disguised with concrete, creating monumental imagery of enfolding and protective arcs.

Castle design also reflected this new honesty of form, with its rounded towers protruding from rounded keeps creating a potent image of defence.

These images and technical developments were confined to the buildings of state and church, making little impact upon residential dwellings. Earring families in Italy might build their houses in the form of solid-based towers with single apartments above and a warning bell on top, but this was imitative building, local security measures rather than any broad response to social needs.

The engine of change remained the church and it was one particular church that signalled the end of the Romanesque period, the emergence of a more coherent architectural style and what we now consider the second half of the Middle Ages.

Gradual improvements to the lord's hall includes the addition of chimneys to the outside walls, the addition of extra storeys for family members, and eventually wings for servants and cooking facilities.

Even so, these improvements took place against a backdrop of civic ruin. Where towns existed at all they no longer had the benefit of the Roman aqueducts, now all ruined and inoperative, with the result that disease was widespread due to lack of hygiene. Only the monasteries, usually sited by spring or stream, were able to maintain higher standards. It was the monasteries too, with their eventual access to medical texts brought back from the East, that would be the agency for a gradual improvement in health.

In terms of building forms, Romanesque remains a loose term, mainly because the familiar phases of any style are complicated by diverse geographical dispersal. The Romanesque forms of Germany, Belgium and Normandy are distinct from those of France, Northern and Southern Italy, or England. The style was applied to castles as well as churches.

gothic

In the year 1144 following one of the fires that accounted for so many wooden-roofed churches, the Abbey Church of St-Denis on the outskirts of Paris was appointed with a new choir under the direction of Abbot Suger, theologian, advisor to kings and highly skilful administrator. In his copious paperwork relating to the rebuilding, he not only carefully documented how the work was to be funded, but also speculated on the importance of appealing to "the dull mind" through spectacularly built forms. This expression of one of architecture's founding principles reaffirmed the inspirational role of building design and established the basis of Gothic architectural thinking. Architecture must once again inspire and uplift, and in its religious expression it must seek to do nothing less than create a magnificent theatre of aspiration through soaring forms and illumination through dazzling pictorial depictions in stained glass.

Ambition without technology is nothing, and of course Abbott Suger's particular ambitions were based upon what could now be achieved. The medieval masons' efforts to solve the problems associated with supporting heavy masonry ceiling vaults across wide spans had always focussed on the fact that such enormous downward and outward pressures tended to deform the walls upon which the vault rested. Any building's vertical supporting walls had to be made immensely thick and heavy in order to contain the vault's outward thrust. The problem was first solved at about 1120 with a number of brilliant innovations of which the first was the ribbed vault, in which arching and intersecting stone ribs support a vaulted ceiling surface made of very thin stone panels. This reduced the weight (and the wall loading) of the ceiling vault, and because the vault's weight was now distributed to the ribs rather than evenly along a continuous wall edge, separate vertical piers could replace continuous thick walls, bringing a new visual lightness. Meanwhile the familiar round arches of the barrel vault were replaced by pointed ones which distributed thrust more economically. The overall result was that Abbot Suger, and indeed anyone else with the means so to do, could specify much thinner walls capable of being opened up with large windows. Larger and taller buildings with complex ground plans were now feasible. In addition, the introduction of flying buttresses made it possible to build very tall, thin-walled buildings with uplifting internal vistas. The psychological possibilities of this were enormous.

Early Gothic

The abbey of Saint-Denis, typifies the first stage of Gothic architecture. The new structural achievements structural elements were exploited in a number of buildings in the prosperous Île-de-France district of Paris, but Saint-Denis is the earliest survivor.

Structures with similarly precise vaulting and an abundance of windows followed. The spectacular Notre-Dame de Paris was begun 1163 and Laon Cathedral started two years later. Soon new refinements were added, such as disguising columns and ribbing as composite strands, and introducing distinctive interior levels to add further dramatic complexity.

A ground-level arcade was topped with one or two galleries and a clerestory (a windowed wall carried higher than surrounding roofs used to light an interior space).

Complex patterns and tracery added to the richness of church interiors and, most significantly, stained glass began to appear in the windows. This basic form of Gothic architecture spread from France throughout Europe to Germany, Italy, England, the Low Countries, Spain, and Portugal.

In England early Gothic churches were distinguished from their French equivalents by a reluctance to abandon thick Romanesque walls, less concern with soaring height and rare use of flying buttresses.

High Gothic

The second phase of Gothic architecture began with the quantum leap of Chartres Cathedral, France. Its unknown architect at a stroke abandoned the previous Gothic approach of achieving visual richness by assembling many small features, and instead chose simpler lines, still recognisably Gothic, but amplified them into a building of staggering scale. This break with tradition was never subsequently pursued to quite the extreme of Chartres, but High Gothic continued by embellishing this new sense of scale with ever more complex effects.

This style, known as Rayonnant (1200–1280) on mainland Europe and Decorated Gothic (1300–75) in England employed elaborate geometrical decoration to the established structural forms of Gothic.

Rayonnant decoration enhanced mouldings and window tracery and took the new form of pinnacles capping buttresses and other exterior elements. However the outstandingly significant innovation of the Rayonnant style was the enormous circular rose window (whose typically radial geometry originally inspired the term Rayonnant) set in the west facade of French cathedrals. Reims, Amiens, Bourges, Chartres and Beauvais cathedrals have outstanding examples.

Later the introduction of Flamboyant tracery changed the character of the French rose window very much in character with the decorative

below Classic early Gothic vaulting in the abbey of the Cathedrale of Saint-Denis, Île de France, Paris

left A fine example of Rayonnant style Gothic, the Cathedral of Notre Dame in Chartres, France, with the tallest surviving Romanesqe steeple

The Rose Window

The Rose Window, also known as the Wheel Window because of its radial, spoke-like segments, is one of the key identifiers of Gothic architecture. These highly decorated, usually stained glass windows, were not entirely unknown before the Gothic period – certainly several Romanesque examples exist, such as that of the 10th century church of Santa Maria in Pomposa, Italy – but it was not until the middle of the 12th century that the idea of making a dramatic, richly-decorated feature out a circular window seemed to catch on. Even then, to begin with, a straightforward rose window was often used more as a trademark than a highly developed feature. Traditionally sited at the west end of the nave and the ends of the transepts, the rose window had to wait until the introduction of developed bar tracery before it reached its pinnacle.

Bar tracery finds its origins in Byzantine effects where pierced marble screens and groups of narrow, arched windows were grouped beneath a single, large arch. The general organisation of a rose window's tracery depended on a series of radiating forms, each tipped by a pointed arch at the outside of the circle. A pierced circle of stone joined the bars between these forms at the centre, while the forms themselves were often designed like small tracery windows with subsidiary, subdividing bars, arches, and circles.

The rose window achieved its greatest medieval popularity in France and the best examples from the High Gothic period are those of the 13th century cathedrals at Amiens, Reims and the famous Notre-Dame in Paris.

extremes of the overall style. Here the radiating elements consisted of a complex web of sinuous bars, featuring the style's characteristic flame shapes. In addition, and as much for structural strength as decorative purpose, a diagonal brace was also added. Beauvais Cathedral (early 16th century) has a good example in the transept.

Although thought of as a speciality of French Gothic architecture, the rose window proved itself a popular export, and from early days could be found throughout Europe. Good examples can be seen in S. Zeno Maggiore at Verona, Italy, Burgos Cathedral Spain, and Lincoln Cathedral, England.

In England the Decorated Gothic style featured newly complex stone window tracery and windows of increased width and height, subdivided into two brightly coloured main sections each further divided by tracery.

Parts of the cloister of Westminster Abbey (c. 1245–69) and the nave and west front of York Minster (c. 1260–1320) are good examples of Decorated Gothic.

Late Gothic.

As the European Rayonnant style evolved into the even more ornate Flamboyant style, in England the Perpendicular style appeared.

Flamboyant Gothic style was defined by the appearance of a distinctive S-shaped curve in stone window tracery, by wall space becoming reduced to the absolute minimum of supports needed, permitting almost unbroken expanse of glass and tracery. Externally, pinnacles, gables, and other intricate details added to the effect of decorative intensity. Although relatively few churches were built exclusively in the Flamboyant style, Notre-Dame d'Épine near Châlons-sur-Marne and Saint-Maclou in Rouen are notable exceptions.

England's contemporaneous Perpendicular Gothic style was identified by larger windows and a predominance of vertical lines in their stone tracery of windows. The distinct storeyed interior, an enduring feature from the early days of the Gothic style, was relinquished in favour of a unifiedvertical expanse. Pointed vaults were gave way to by fan vaults which extended from slender columns. Gloucester Cathedral (14th and 15th centuries) and King's College Chapel, Cambridge (1446-1515) are good examples of the Perpendicular Gothic style.

right The cloisters of the cathedral at Gloucester, England

above The breathtaking interior of the choir in the Dom – cathedral – in Cologne, Germany

right Cologne Cathedral, towering above the post-modern municipal art gallery in the foreground

Cologne Cathedral

Cologne's cathedral dominates the city in every respect. A vast, towering building it represents the culmination of many of the concerns of Gothic architecture, despite the fact that in its epic ambitions it overreached itself – only the choir was fully completed in the middle ages. This, though, stands as testament both to the faith that generated many of the medieval cathedrals (no one working on a given building could assume that it would be completed in his lifetime) and to the enduring appeal of the Gothic style.

After an earlier cathedral on the site was destroyed by fire in 1248, a new one was ordered to be built in the Gothic style, after the fashion of neighbouring France's great cathedrals. The choir was completed in 1320 and consecrated two years later. Building continued for over 200 years, until it was abandoned, unfinished. Work did not resume until 1842, by which time it was the age of the Gothic Revival. Continuation was due to the efforts of Sulpiz Boisserée, one of the most active and enthusiastic of early Gothic Revivalists. It was he who received the moral support of Goethe and the financial backing of King Frederick William III, who ordered the preservation of the building. The task of completion was begun in 1842, at the command of King Frederick William IV, and was finally to be completed in 1880. Despite air raid damage in the Second World War, the cathedral was fully restored and stands today an extraordinary monument to the power of the Gothic ideal, its twin towers soaring some 156 metres feet above the modern city centre.

The cathedral's 14th-century stained-glass windows in the choir are exceptional by any standards and the cathedral houses art treasures (including a triptych by Stefan Lochner, of the Cologne school, *The Adoration of the Magi*, from c. 1440) and a shrine, allegedly containing relics of the Magi, transported there from Italy in 1164. Apart from its religious significance this shrine represents one of the finest existing examples of medieval goldwork.

Near the cathedral's south side lies a relic of Cologne's ancient past: the mosaic floor of a banquet hall in a great Roman villa, discovered during excavations near the cathedral in 1941. The floor is now incorporated in the city's Römisch-Germanisches Museum.

san gimignano, tuscany

San Gimignano

It still has its city walls, gates, and 14 of its original 72 towers remain intact. San Gimignano is a virtual museum of Gothic architecture, its most important monuments being the Palazzo del Popolo – containing the civic museum and art gallery and the Collegiata – and the church of Sant' Agostino with frescoes showing scenes from the life of St. Augustine. The town is laid out in linear form with the familiar gate at each end. Two large piazzas were designed for the marketplace and a collection of civic buildings. The limestone towers, their original number depleted not by war or neglect but by poor foundations, typify the urban strongholds of feuding families that can be seen all over Italy.

Secular Concerns

The predominance of the church and religious building styles in the Middle Ages is overwhelming. We look in vain for any coherent or sustained developments either in the advance of towns and cities or great refinement in ordinary living conditions.

However, the high aspirations of Romanesque and Gothic architecture reaffirm the fundamental considerations of how the built environment both prescribes and responds to change, aspiration and technology.

What is more, it is true to say that throughout the Middle Ages technological change was having a gradual but lasting impact upon daily life as well as upon the development of great religious monuments.

Towards the end of the Gothic period there was also evidence – localised to be sure, but significant – of the national characteristics of the Gothic style being reinterpreted in the homes of the rich.

The dazzling array merchants' homes along the Grand Canal in Venice combine the Gothic principle of relieving great masses through visually light arrangements of pierced masonry, with a decidedly Islamic look that bears testimony to Venice's long trading history.

A very French version of the Gothic ideal can be seen in the house of a wealthy merchant, Jacques Coeur, at Bourges in France. Built around the middle of the 15th century, it features a highly-decorated façade, fretted balconies and a whole wealth of architectural quotations from late French Gothic cathedral architecture.

English secular architecture too had its excursions into local Gothic styles, as evidenced by another country house, this time that of wealthy wool merchant William Grevel in Chipping Campden, Gloucestershire. Here identifiable elements of the English Perpendicular – slender stone mullions in the bow window – are translated into a simple residential building.

Medieval Technology

Important early advances included the 9th century discovery of how to harness water power for the task of flour milling. Water power, it was discovered, could also be used to drive rudimentary machinery, in some cases radically changing the productivity of certain manufacturing processes such as cloth working. Improvements in harness design meant that horses could replace oxen for certain ploughing and carting tasks. Windmills were developed and became very popular in appropriate regions, and by the 13th century, mining techniques had improved to such an extent that new rich sources of iron, copper, tin, and lead were suddenly accessible in mining regions all over Europe where resources had previously been thought to be exhausted or depleted. Sustainable resources became a real issue in other areas too. Timber, once believed to be an inexhaustible material, was in short supply, being needed for shipbuilding and so previously wooden implements, even household ones, were suddenly being manufactured from iron. Houses built of brick or stone were increasingly common. These sometimes featured the glass windows and chimneys formerly found only in the houses of the wealthy. Domestic furniture became more sophisticated, employing better joinery than the old crude benches and tables. Metal cooking pots, glass containers, and wheel-turned pottery came into widespread use too. By the 15th century records show that in these and other areas, the eating habits of the rich were filtering down to a much wider population.

The Re-emergence of The City

The early part of the Middle Ages had marked a low point in the fortunes of the city. Monasteries had to some extent hi-jacked the city's function, and the feudal system had continued to maintain some sort of workable hierarchy, but the basic human need to create cities re-emerged almost as soon as conditions began to improve after the dark ages. With the exception of a few major conurbations like Paris or London, these re-emerging cities were of small populations, modest, pragmatic and fragmented, and generally fell into one of three physical forms. The most basic of these was simply an enclosed cluster of buildings that had grown up at the side of a road, enclosed but with gates at either end. An informal external clearance provided a makeshift marketplace. Another type usually took the shape of an irregular circle, informally defined and enclosed by a wall that itself was shaped by the local landscape or land ownership. A third, based on the lineaments of an old Roman plan, was rectangular with an internal grid pattern defined by the rectilinear shape.

Whatever its geometry the medieval city of the 11th and 12th centuries owed more to the organic responses of Islamic settlements than the formal organisation of Rome. Piecemeal expansion was reflected in ever-moving city walls which would be extended on an ad hoc basis. Internal planning was hardly worthy of the name although a form of logic did govern them. Narrow streets and overcrowded conditions were the inevitable result of a clamouring to get in and away from the dangers uncertainties of feudal life outside. Very little consideration was given to public needs to begin with, usually because of the vested interests of landowners, although eventually a form of civic pride emerged that carried with it something of the devotional intensity of the age. Just as religion drove all major medieval architecture, religious-like fervour made these medieval towns objects of worship by their citizens, venerated places with saints as patrons and a brand of urban evangelism instead of civic pride. Eventually a wealth of facilities emerged in hard-won spaces at the city centres of the 13th and 14th centuries: churches and city halls; hospitals and food stores; campaniles and universities.

These cities did not survive the ages well, except in parts of Italy which was much slower than the rest of Europe to join the industrial age. For this reason the town of San Gimignano, built on a ridge in Tuscany, is important as an almost miraculously preserved Italian medieval town.

Out Of The Middle Ages

Italy is an appropriate place to leave the Gothic adventure since it was the site of the next great stylistic change. Italy had always had something of a classical feeling for architecture; if classicism was to be reborn anywhere Italy was the most likely place. Like all architectural styles Renaissance emerged rather more seamlessly than our later labels might suggest, and its early stages of course overlapped with the final stages of late Gothic.

6

renaissance italy

6

florentine revival

Rinascimento was a word already in use in Italian writings of the early 15th century. It was applied to the reapplication of the standards and images of ancient Rome. So, for once, we have a label at least in use by those with whom history associates it even if the modern concept of The Renaissance as a two-century-long period of exuberant revival and reinvention in Italian architecture and art was the invention of 19th century scholars.

The Renaissance began not in Rome, as might be expected of an Italian revival of classical values, but in Florence. During the 14th and early 15th centuries the political situation in Rome was unsympathetic to the arts in general and architecture in particular. Florence, however, effectively ruled by the Medici family, was economically prosperous, politically very stable and furthermore enjoyed the lavish patronage of that family. One hundred and fifty miles away in Milan were the Sforza, a family that ruled the duchy sporadically from 1450 to 1535 and who were also prominent patrons of the arts. Wealth, enlightenment and stability, then, were the necessary requirements for a rediscovery of the great cultural values of the past, and Florence, more than any other Italian city, could claim them.

Most shifts of cultural emphasis need a single galvanizing event to fix and focus them, and whilst Florence already had all of the credentials needed to spearhead a cultural revival, it was the creation of a single feature for a great Florentine building that gave the Renaissance its initial spark. The building was Florence Cathedral, the feature its dome and its architect Filippo Brunelleschi.

The Dome of Florence Cathedral

Florence Cathedral had started construction in 1296, but by 1418 it had been halted by the immense technical problems posed by constructing an eight-sided vault of pointed curvature – without the use of any exterior buttressing – above an enormous octagonal space. Inheriting such an ambitious untried design had led to many bitter arguments by several generations of architects. In 1418 another competition was announced, this time for models of inventions to help build the dome. Again both Brunelleschi and Ghiberti entered, but this time Brunelleschi won, whose entry showed that the dome could be constructed according to an ancient Roman technique of placing the brickwork in herringbone patterns between a framework of stone beams.

Brunelleschi's dome began construction in 1420 using his method for carrying out the complicated construction process, which was in itself a major engineering achievement.

Brunelleschi had invented a complicated wooden form around which the eight-sided dome was to be built as a double shell, inner and outer, in order to save weight. The ribs of the dome were tied together with a series of reinforcing timber bands which were clamped with iron. A cupola on top, which might seem like nothing more than a visual conceit, actually operated as a masonry anchor, with its weight helping to hold together the pointed dome beneath.

Brunelleschi became chief architect of the project in 1420, a post he held until his death in 1446.

Brunelleschi 1377–1446

Filippo Brunelleschi, born in Florence in 1377, initially trained as a goldsmith and sculptor, applying for registration in the Arte della Seta and receiving the official designation of Master in 1401. In one of history's happy accidents Brunelleschi's bid to win a competition to create the bronze reliefs for the door of the Baptistery of Florence failed. His entry, a panel depicting The Sacrifice of Isaac is a highly dramatic and much admired piece of sculpture, but the competition winner was Lorenzo Ghiberti and the highly ambitious Brunelleschi immediately departed sculpture for architecture.

It is indicative of the free-thinking cultural spirit of Florence at this time that the notion of narrow, self-referential disciplines was unknown. As an inquisitive trainee architect, Brunelleschi was still open all of the visual arts, and so it was that around 1410, he rediscovered the fine art principles of linear-perspective construction that had been well known to the Greeks and Romans but lost along with so much else during medieval times.

Brunelleschi illustrated his findings with two exemplary paintings of contemporary Florentine streets scenes, demonstrating the principle of a single vanishing point on a two-dimensional representation of a three-dimensional scene, where all parallel appear to converge. He also showed the relationship between distance and the illusion of objects becoming smaller as they get further away from the observer.

Such notions today seem a matter of obvious common sense, but the visual arts of Italy before Brunelleschi demonstrate that the flat, stylized, unrealistic depiction of scenes was the unvarying 'reality' accepted as figurative art.

From this point on Fillippo Brunelleschi's contemporary artists were able to produce illusions of three-dimensional space and tangible objects, so that the work of art was no longer a stylization but a mirror to the real world.

Brunelleschi's breakthrough was later formalized in the writings of his contemporary, the architect Leon Battista Alberti, in 1435.

So, whilst still in his early 30s, Brunelleschi had already produced a masterwork in sculpture and change the course of pictorial representation forever. His architectural career had not yet begun. When it did it was to produce an even more momentous piece of work.

above   One of the landmarks of Renaissance architecture, in every sense of the word, the Brunelleschi dome of Florence Cathedral

pienza, toscana

Other Buildings

He also made other major contributions to the early Renaissance. His Ospedale degli Innocenti, or Foundling Hospital, built in 1421 is a simple and beautiful building with echoes of Italian Romanesque and late Gothic architecture. However it was the hospital's façade that distinguished it from previous styles by providing an elegant reworking of classical features: pilasters, friezes and Corinthian capitals all reintroduced with a great sense of visual harmony.

Brunelleschi became the leading architect in Florence, profiting like many others from the patronage of the Medici family who commissioned him to design the sacristy of San Lorenzo and the Basilica of San Lorenzo itself. Once again Brunelleschi helped to define early Renaissance style, this time by embellishing the traditional basilican church form with his reinventions of classical features seamlessly incorporated.

Another wealthy Florentine family, the Pazzi, commissioned Brunelleschi to design a chapel in the cloisters of the Church of Santa Croce. The result was a definitive building in the Renaissance canon. For it Brunelleschi used mathematical modules and geometric formulas, creating a square covered by a dome. The centre of the chapel was a circle beneath the dome – a revolutionary departure from the traditional nave-and-aisle arrangement. Decorative bands of grey stone mark off the walls in a continuation of a cool, considered style defined by geometry in the service of visual harmony.

Brunelleschi created several more major buildings, among them the churches of Santo Spirito and Santa Maria degli Angeli, both in Florence. Of these Santa Maria degli Angeli was perhaps his most revolutionary design since it was based on a central octagon leading to eight chapels, with a 16-sided exterior.

Secular Buildings

It is claimed by an early biographer that Brunelleschi built many palaces. No proven evidence of these exists, although it is likely that he acted as advisor if not architect on residential buildings of the wealthy.

He did create some military architecture, although again it remains unclear to what extent he advised or designed fortifications for Vicopisano, Pisa, Rencine, Rimini, and Pesaro. He is also known to have contributed to an ambitious scheme to divert the Arno River and therby make the city of Lucca into an island.

He remained professionally active until the end of his life, and died in Florence in 1446. He was buried in Florence Cathedral.

social background

Brunelleschi is important because, although he obviously belonged to the early Renaissance, helping to define its concerns and ambitions, his career also encapsulates much of what was to follow. He was an individual genius, but individual geniuses alone do not start major cultural movements. The ground must be prepared by other circumstances for such things to happen.

At the end of the Gothic period, society was changing due to a variety of developments, some social, some technological.

Primarily, commerce and banking had become respectable, no longer winning the disapproval of the church whose own fortunes increasingly depended upon skilful management and investment. Commerce and banking made Florence rich and the rich families of Florence – the Medicis and others – became the new aristocracy, with commercial empires throughout Europe and a very different view of the world from that of the feudal noblemen who had preceded them

Better navigational equipment and superior shipbuilding skills had extended the limits of the known world, not only helping to extend and accelerate commercial activity, but also changing the philosophical outlook of a Europe which could now access the hitherto uncharted lands China, India and America by sea.

Gunpowder had been invented, further obliging countries to reassess the nature of conflicts which would no longer be conducted exclusively on the old terms and therefore obliged a reassessment of international affairs.

top left The Pious II piazza in Pienza, near Sienna, demonstrating some of the enduring qualities of Renaissance architecture

bottom left Pienza as depicted by the painter Piero della Francesca as 'The City of God'

below Inside the church of Santo Spirito in Florence, considered one of Brunelleschi's finest works

Alberti 1404–1472

Through his writing and his buildings, Leone Battista Alberti (1404–72) succeeded in creating a system of simple proportion that would be followed for centuries.

In an extraordinarily rich life Alberti appears to have tried and succeeded at so much that he might almost have embodied the impossible ideal of the Renaissance man. Writer, musician, mathematician, painter and athlete he was, most famously, an architectural theorist. He described architectural beauty as 'the harmony and concord of all the parts achieved in such a manner that nothing could be added or taken away or altered except for the worse'.

Although, as we shall see, the primary impulses of Renaissance architectural thought were lofty rather than workaday, Alberti's written contribution to town planning were eminently practical. In his *De re Ædificatoria* (Ten Books of Architecture) he addressed the eternal problem of which parts of the city's fabric should be accentuated and which parts hidden. 'The beauty of the city' he wrote, 'will be greatly enhanced if various artisan workshops are built in the city districts and areas appropriate to them. There will be bankers, painters and goldsmiths around the square; near to them shops with aromatic spices and merchandise, tailor shops and those which are considered important. Ugly merchandise should be secluded in more distant places'.

Alberti transformed the Gothic church of S. Francesco, Rimini, into a memorial to a local family, a building which subsequently came to be known as Tempio Malatestiano and consisting of a marble shell that completely encased the old building. He was the papal advisor on the restoration of Rome, and innovator of another key element in Renaissance architectural thought, that of harmonic proportions.

below Leone Alberti's beautifully proportioned facade of the church of Santa Maria Novella in Florence

In 1450 the biggest invention of all – Gutenberg's movable type printing press – would enable the spread of all new ideas and discoveries to a wider audience than ever before.

Perhaps more influential than any of these developments was the general idea of change that they represented. A new age was being born and one which architecture would play a crucial role. Brunelleschi's discoveries of classical technologies prefigured one of the key aspects of the Renaissance: renewed access to the intellectual treasures of the past.

Federigo da Montefeltro was Duke of Urbino, a cultured and learned man who collected one of the best libraries in Italy, employing many scribes over a period of years to copy out numerous texts. These texts were to provide an intellectual equivalent to the physical voyages of discovery of the Renaissance, giving contemporary academics access to classical texts and allowing the spread of ideas, most notably through a group of teachers who became known as the Humanists. Humanism was belief in the high potential of human nature as opposed to religious values. It encouraged the active, rather than the contemplative life, and a faith in the republican ideal. It fostered individualism, and the ideal of the all-round man, in equal parts statesman, poet, warrior and scholar.

The importance of those revived classical texts was of immense value to the development of architectural thinking in Renaissance Italy.

By the 1480s Vitruvius' ten books of architecture had re-emerged and proved highly influential in an environment where architects were elevated by the spirit of the age from gifted craftsmen to intellectuals with a mission to elevate the human spirit through the arts in general and particularly through inspirational building design. Typifying this new approach to architecture was Leone Battista Alberti.

The principle of harmonic proportions appeared in Alberti's façade for the Italian Gothic-style church of S. Maria Novella in Florence. The façade is entirely covered with an inlay of different coloured marbles and is based upon an geometric series of squares that correspond exactly to the ideal proportions of antiquity.

This and Alberti's other buildings proved worthy successors to the work of his near contemporary Brunelleschi, although quite distinct from them Brunelleschi had effortlessly bridged Gothic and emergent Renaissance styles. Alberti gave Renaissance architecture a new direction.

rome & the high renaissance

Rome, which might have been thought the natural birthplace of this movement of humanism, rediscovered classicism, and enlightened patronage, was the second Italian city to subscribe to the Renaissance. By the time it did, the style had developed into the brief period we now call High Renaissance.

High Renaissance architecture first appeared at Rome at the beginning of the 16th century. The emphasis of power and culture had drifted from Florence to Rome mainly because papal ambitions to acquire more secular power meant that a wealthy church rather than wealthy merchants could now be the great patrons of the arts. Few of those whose received their

Science & Technology

The Renaissance encouraged considerable technological advance, at least in the immediate service of its own ends.

Still guided by largely medieval ideas about the natural world, the engineers and scientists of of the 15th and 16th centuries made considerable advances in the service of the pragmatic spirit of the age. For example, the principles governing the motion of bodies in space were explored with a new urgency not out of any abstract love of knowledge for its own sake but because the invention of gunpowder and an increased use of artillery made such issues of pressing practical concern. Gun manufacturing processes also had implications for metallurgy and fortification. Geometry was not just an abstract concept but of practical value in planning towns in a rational way. Alchemy too was stimulated by a scarceness of precious metals. Most significant of all was the communications revolution.

Brought about by the refinement of movable metal type, ostensibly by Johannes Gutenberg but probably equally by two of his contemporaries, Peter Schöffer and Johann Fust.

By 1500 the presses of Europe had generated at least 7 million books increasing the opportunities for enlightenment immeasurably and changing the balances of power and control for all time.

Harmonic Proportions

The theory of harmonic proportions was developed in ancient times but rediscovered and exploited by Alberti in Renaissance Italy. The theory contrived to draw visual lessons from the perceptible laws of music whereby musical strings of varying length produce differences of an octave, a fifth or a fourth depending on respective lengths of a half, two-thirds and a quarter. It was extrapolated from this that rooms conforming to the same ratios would automatically enjoy a harmonious appearance.

patronage were local, but arrival in Rome often seems to have conferred a new focus and in turn, new heights of achievement.

Donato Bramante, had already established for himself an architectural reputation in Milan. Once in Rome, where he arrived in 1499, there was a change in his work which was to make him the dominant architect of the High Renaissance.

The Tempietto (1502), or small chapel, next to San Pietro in Montorio, typifies the beginnings of the High Renaissance style. Modelled upon the ancient temples of Vesta at Rome and Tivoli and placed on what is thought to be site of the martyrdom of St. Peter, the Tempietto is a circular drum-like structure with a colonnade surrounding a small interior sanctuary. Outside it was two storeys high with a Doric colonnade forming the first storey. Above stands a dome so perfectly proportioned and in keeping with the rest of the structure that The Tempietto has become a classic building endlessly copied from everywhere from Washington D.C. in The Capitol, to Hawksmoor's Mausoleum at Castle Howard, Yorkshire, England.

Bramante became fascinated with perspective illusionism and explored it in a building (now much altered) for Pope Julius II in 1505, the Cortile del Belvedere. This was part of an ambitious plan to remodel the Vatican. So ambitious was it in its effort to link the Vatican Palace with a pre-existing villa some 300 yards away, that it was never completed in Bramante's lifetime and later became so altered that only the original drawings give any idea of its intentions.

These were to recreate some of the more hedonistic expressions of Imperial Rome in a rich complex consisting of garden, sculpture court and theatre. Corridors, niches, triumphal arches, giant pilasters and fountains all reflected Bramante's ambitions to create an architectural expression of the idea of reason subduing nature for the entertainment of man. It was to be the first of innumerable such exercises that would extend all the way from Renaissance Rome to the court of Louis XIV of France and the Palace of Versailles.

left The courtyard of the Cancelleria Palace in Rome built between 1486 and 1498 and Donato Bramante

right Bramante's Tempietto San Petro in Montorio, Rome

tempietto, rome

St Peter's, Rome

Early in 1505 Pope Julius II began to consider the question of a tomb for himself that would be appropriate to his idea of the power and nobility of his position. The sculptor Michelangelo soon presented a great project for a freestanding tomb, but such a monument required a proper setting. The Renaissance artist and biographer Giorgio Vasari claimed that the question of an appropriate location for this projected tomb brought to the Pope's mind the idea of rebuilding St. Peter's, which was in very poor condition. Bramante, therefore, prepared plans for a monumental church late in 1505.

In its monumental scale and ambition this, the latest attempt to complete one of the world's greatest churches was daring even by the confident standards of the Renaissance. Bramante's fundamental plan was to alter the shape of a building that was still in essence a church built shaped in a centralized way over the tomb of the Prince of The Apostles.

Bramante proposed a gargantuan version of his own Tempietto of 1502; this translated into a Greek Cross each of whose arms terminates in

an apse and a huge dome on a colonnaded drum over the point of crossing. Subsidiary domes would appear on the corners of the cross and tall bell towers would flank the main façade.

This radical plan meant that there would be no nave for liturgical processions, nor would there be a focal point to site the main altar. For these reasons Bramante was later obliged to lengthen one of the arms of his Greek cross. The proposed main dome was to be supported on four monumental piers tied together by arches at their crossing and buttressed by smaller arches and walls. The ancient Roman practice of using masonry supported by cement had already been used by Bramante in his Tempietto, and would here be used again on an epic scale for St Peter's Dome.

It is perhaps fitting that Bramante's proposal for St Peter's, although not accepted in its entirety and, in practical building terms, only just begun when its architect died, would determine its final appearance more than any other. Theory and concept outlived realization, and not only in at St

Peter's: it influenced church architecture for another 100 years. The completion of St Peter's involved many plans and disputes about structural theory. Bramante was already an old man when construction started on his plan, and subsequent contributors (drawn in true Renaissance style from many cultural compass points) included Raphael, Michelangelo, Vignola and Maderna.

However it was Giuliano da Sangallo who, at around the end of the 16th century, advanced St Peter's in any significant way. He strengthened the pillars, completed construction of the nave vaulting and, most significantly, altered the dome from classical hemisphere to ribbed segment. This change of form allowed an increase in height of 9 metres or so. Continuing this architectural relay race, Michelangelo took over the design of the dome, giving it the final form that would be realized by Giacomo della Porta and Domenico Fontana. In doing so Michelangelo returned to Florence Cathedral, the beginning of the Renaissance, and Brunelleschi's solution for that dome. The result is a double-shell dome, its ribs held together with chains and its interior made largely of brick. The resulting structure serves mainly as a visual focus for the distant observer, identifying an important location and reinforcing Rome's religious significance.

What then was Michelangelo's contribution to a dome that had effectively been created a century before? Chiefly it was to give a sculptural quality to St Peter's and to enhance its sense of drama through its spatial qualities as much as its scale. Also, Michelangelo spent the majority of his time working on the lower parts of the building. In yet another return to the past, he rejected the work of his immediate predecessors, returning to the scheme of the original designer, Bramante. He returned too to the initial Greek Cross form plan and removed a number of later small decorative elements.

Michelangelo was, however, prepared to modify certain aspects of Bramante's interior, unifying the internal space even more.

Much of the work that the famous sculptor and painter oversaw in his declining years was concerned with the curved wall behind the altar, where supports of dramatically contrasting scale suggest a dynamic upward movement, part of an elaborate sculptural *tour de force*.

At the base of the dome Michelangelo specified a columned walkway where the tops of the columns were tied to the dome by beams, but with the unusual feature of no actual horizontal links connecting the tops of the columns. This results in another imaginative sculptural effect, with the columns having the effect of flying buttresses to support the dome's downward thrust.

Michelangelo did not revive Bramante's subsidiary domes or the flanking bell towers. Instead he carried the outer walls to the same height all round, relieving them with the massive coupled Corinthian pilasters that had been devised by Bramante for the supports of the dome inside.

So, with relatively few subsequent alterations, the design of St Peter's was concluded: an epic architectural co-operative effort which, despite trials and tribulations, resulted in a classic High Renaissance building originally conceived by Julius II as a monument by Bramante to eclipse the finest buildings of ancient Rome.

left The interior nave in the Basilica of Saint Peter's in the Vatican

above An interior view of the breathtaking dome of Saint Peter's

below Saint Peter's and the Vatican in the middle of modern-day Rome

Andrea Palladio 1508–1580

The most influential architect of the time and region, though was Andrea Palladio, a man who, like Vitruvius in the 1st century, would bequeath his heirs not only buildings but enduring theories too.

In Venice Palladio's first design was for the façade of San Pietro di Castello (1558). By the1560s he was working on Venetian monastic buildings for Santa Maria della Carità and on the refectory and cloisters of San Giorgio Maggiore.

Then in 1562 he designed the façade for San Francesco della Vigna, at Venice, originally constructed to Sansovino's designs of 1534 but still unfinished. Palladio's façade became a pattern for classical churches, with the visual disparity of a high nave with lower aisles, a problem he resolved with a double-plane solution of temple fronts.

Prior to this successful conclusion of a life in architecture, Palladio had already executed the body of work that would make him famous in another country and another century. Palladio's villas for wealthy clients were built for the rich along lines based on the Roman villa as Palladio understood it to have existed from the writings of Vitruvius. Palladio's clients, increasingly prosperous and with income often related to land reclamation, required summer residences or distinguished rural headquarters. To address this need Palladio devised the prototype plan of Villa Trissino. It was a flexible plan which in its summer residence version is most famously seen in a belvedere for Giulio Capra, the Villa Rotonda, near Vicenza. The Villa Trissino at Meledo, of the same type, was intended to have curved wings extending from the main portico, an effect usually omitted when the villa was for a gentleman with working land. The Villa Trissino was never built but became immortal when Palladio featured it in his published treatise on architecture.

The same temple fronts that he deployed so imaginatively in later churches like San Francesco della Vigna, Palladio adapted to the façades of his villas because he believed them to be both dignified and based upon a genuine Roman domestic model – the Roman house which, he assumed, must have shared the same pedimented porticoes as the temples.

At the Villa Thiene (c.1550) at Quinto, Palladio began a more ambitious house based upon a reconstructed Roman villa, and this is also to be seen in his published treatise although it was never actually completed. At the Villa Sarego, 1569, at Santa Sofia he tried a similar introverted complex although that too was not completed. These two buildings suggest a departure from the villa model not only because of the inclusion of a two-storey rusticated and a courtyard effect, but also because in its more complex scheme it suggests the emergence of a new form not fully explored.

When Palladio died he left many unfinished buildings, including a Basilica in Vicenza and the two churches at Venice. These were continued by his followers Vincenzo Scamozzi and O. Bertotti-Scamozzi with amendments of which Palladio would probably have disapproved.

Towards the end of his highly productive life, Palladio published *I Quattro Libri dell'Architettura*, a summary of what he had gleaned from classical architecture liberally illustrated with his own schemes. It was meant to be his response to Vitruvius, whose writings far eclipsed his built achievement. If Palladio was seeking immortality, he succeeded better than he could have known. Inigo Jones introduced Palladian architecture into England after a visit to Italy and perusal of Palladio's writings. From there came the Queen's House at Greenwich, completed in 1635, the Banqueting House at Whitehall, completed in 1622 and the Queen's Chapel at St. James Palace of 1623. By the 18th century a revival of Palladianism in England spread to Italy and from there to the rest of Europe and the American colonies.

In addition to St Peter's, Michelangelo produced a number of adventurous and usually highly sculptural buildings towards the end of his life. He also introduced many innovations by demonstrating, seemingly effortlessly, how classical elements could be integrated into contemporary architecture without looking nostalgic or conservative.

Always forward looking, he worked in an adventurous way that would, to future architectural historians, seem to make him more naturally part of the period after his own, when Renaissance turned into Baroque.

outwards from rome

Born in Florence and reaching its full flowering in Rome, Italian Renaissance architecture also spread to many other Italian cities before extending itself even further afield. This process was hastened by the sudden decline of Rome when it was invaded by the mercenary forces of Emperor Charles V on May 6, 1527. Forcing the pope to flee to the Castel Sant'Angelo, the army sacked the city and effectively terminated what had become the mainspring of the High Renaissance.

One of the main focuses of the now displaced architectural activity was Venice and the Veneto. There Michele Sanmicheli and Jacopo Sansovino helped to establish the High Renaissance style. Sanmicheli became the driving force behind the construction of a new city at Verona. Sansovino, a Florentine who had worked on St Peter's, went to Venice where he was appointed chief architect of San Marco and was responsible for fine buildings such as the Libreria di san Marco (begun 1536).

below The Villa Rotonda at Vicenza, Italy, built for Giulio Capra by Palladio

Any discussion of the Renaissance in Italy must leave the impression that this was architecturally an elitist movement, driven by intellectual aspirations, power, money and the church. It must also seem that it was a period of individuals, many of them apparently gifted to an almost superhuman degree. If it seems so, perhaps it was so. Certainly the emphasis of history is the same as the emphasis of the time: humanism, the cult of the individual and culture led by enlightened gentility through religious monuments and epic schemes.

However, equally important – perhaps uniquely so – was Renaissance Italy's vigorous and thoughtful attempt to bridge the chasm between itself and classical antiquity. There were relatively few attempts to wallow in a fictional past, even though ancient Rome must have seemed a mythical place. Intellectual rigour, not sentiment, was what drove the best architectural minds forward and if, with the notable exception of Palladio, they were less interested in secular buildings than mighty churches, more concerned with courting the wealthy and influential than improving the day to day fabric of the city for everyone else, then that too was part of Renaissance thinking.

In fact during the Renaissance the resurgence of urban life begun in the Middle Ages continued with many incremental improvements. Banking and commercial enterprise not only flourished but helped to make the Renaissance happen in the first place. In terms of political geography, city-states and local principalities continued to replace the diminishing powers of empire and church although within the new divisions there were few changes of social order. Also the 'label' theory favoured by historians has left us with insufficient evidence of how day to day life inter-reacted with the more exalted activity of the Renaissance thinkers and doers. In the final analysis the *rinascimento* was in the arts and intellect, not the social fabric.

Mannerism

The Renaissance in Italy itself finally became muted and in many instances transformed by a relatively brief period known as Mannerism which historically extended from the time of Michelangelo to the end of the 16th century. More fully expressed in sculpture and painting than in architecture, and as much a symptom as a distinct style, Mannerism tended to encourage reactions against those aspects of Renaissance culture which were now becoming over-familiar and jaded. Classical details and features were jolted out of context for effect, sometimes skilfully, sometimes in a way that makes the word mannerism seem appropriate in its most pejorative sense.

Michelangelo introduced this new mood with a playful use of giant orders, magnified versions of classical columns that might span three storeys or an entire façade.

Michelangelo explored such possibilities on a grand scale in a project designed to rationalise a group of near derelict palaces surrounding the Capitol in Rome. Here Michelangelo brought his robust vision to a monumental piece of town planning that was to create one of Rome's best vistas. A wide, shallow-incline ramp was inserted between the antique statues of Castor and Pollux and led to a diamond-shaped piazza in which

he laid a radiant star in white stone in an oval pool of ripples. This idiosyncratic shape was a complete departure from the accepted palette of imagery in Renaissance architecture. So too was the sculptor's architectural treatment of the building at the head of the square, The Palace of the Senators and its two flanking palaces. Here Michelangelo introduced his giant versions of the classical orders and pilasters. Spanning several storeys, these self-consciously enlarged fragments of the past signified the end of a phase of a cultural deference and heralded the beginning of a more independent spirit.

From this point on – around the early 1500s – it became much more common to rail against the classical formulae that had fed the Renaissance. This occasionally produced some jokey effects.

Giulio Romano was a pupil of Raphael and a supremely competent architect, but he was not above slipping in dissonant architectural details like an anomalous keystone in an architrave (keystones belong only in arches, not architraves) in the courtyard of the Palazzo del Tè in Mantua. The intention was to shock and alarm, even though the structural integrity of the building was in no way threatened. The whole concept of the Palazzo del Tè was anyway full of allusion and illusion. An island building commissioned simply as a place to stay while the client, the Gonzaga family, conducted its occasional horse breeding business, the villa became a complex bestowed with the title of palace. Under Romano it became a virtuoso box of architectural tricks in which the classical was subverted with a mixture of effects both comic and supremely skilful.

There was a more serious side to architectural Mannerism too though. Baldassare Peruzzi began the Palazzo Massimo alle Colonne in Rome in 1532, and his rebellion took the form of a façade that was curved – an unheard of departure from the norm. Many other unusual effects were incorporated and the overall effect is one of bold irregularity extremely well-managed and curiously impressive: a maverick treatment that is something more than an attempt to shock.

Giacomo Barozzi da Vignola was a Mannerist with a more controlled and restrained approach. He designed a country retreat for Pope Julius III which in its organisation abandoned the classical idea of fixed viewpoints and calm vistas replacing them with hidden features and aspects that suddenly revealed themselves. He also created a notable church for the Jesuit order Il Gesù which became an established type and much copied. Following the death of his patron Pope Julius, Vignola worked mainly for the Farnese family, building the huge Palazzo Farnese at Caprarola.

Mannerism was a minor movement, yet significant because it showed what few in the High Renaissance had thought possible, that restrained classical buildings could outstay their welcome. The mood in Italy was ready for a change in the way architecture would develop. Unlike Mannerism which only occasionally rose above the level of an in-joke, the next wave was one that engaged directly with politics, religion and power, even if it seemed at first just another exercise in style.

right Palladio's Church of San Giorgio Maggiore in Venice

san giorgio maggiore, venice

7

baroque exuberance

St Pauls Cathedral, London

above The facade of the Jesuit church of Il Gesù, Rome, by the great Mannerist Giacomo da Vignola

out of classicism into style

The Renaissance in Italy lasted for 200 years during which an extraordinary cultural trick was worked. Centuries of ignorance, terror and barbarism had been followed by a turning back of the clock – the revival of the values of a lost civilisation in the fresh context of an affluent new age. What is more, the effect had not been that of beautifying a corpse but that of a genuine revival in which substance and spirit had flourished together. Subsequently the mood of the Renaissance had also spread abroad, with predictable domestic variants, usually achieved through an uneasy hybrid of pure Italian Renaissance with some prevalent local form or forms.

As for the city shape and fabric themselves, overshadowed in the history books by the lofty aspirations of great architecture, it is not that development ceased, rather than the patchwork of European states continued to exist on a variety of levels. The most primitive rural settlements could still be found all over Europe, but a miscellany of more sophisticated settlements existed too, clustered around monasteries, or developed into highly organised trading centres. What had stalled was any coherent and widespread philosophy like those of Greece and Rome, to develop towns to a set of principles that would serve a central ideal; there was in short, no great empire.

Where wealthy cities were created it was often the result of local circumstances with local agendas. Whilst cities like Renaissance Rome and Florence contained great wealth and commitment to architecture, their adherence to Roman civic principles remained selective in that it was mainly directed towards the great buildings of church and state, not town planning at an everyday level.

The architectural history of the Renaissance and periods that immediately followed, was a history of grand concepts and exceptional individual practitioners.

Baroque Beginnings

The new dominant style would be termed Baroque, to begin with a term even more unambiguously disparaging than Mannerism had been. In all probability it derived from the Italian word *barocco,* (a medieval term in philosophy used to describe an obstacle in logic), 'Baroque' had come to connote any unnecessarily complex or involuted thought process.

So was Baroque architecture unnecessarily complex or involuted? To find out we need to look not only at the phenomenon itself but also at some of the forces that helped to bring it into being.

From 1600 to about 1750 architecture, painting, and sculpture became much more closely entwined than ever before. The object was to create dramatic decorative ensembles, with the roles of architecture and sculpture becoming almost interdependent to provide rich settings for paintings which became more illusionistic in character. This was the Baroque style and it was a celebratory architecture composed of vivid colours, luxurious materials, hidden light sources and sensual surface textures. Most of all Baroque space was about motion and dynamism, with calculated effects of direction and movement – a clear reaction against the coolly static space of the High Renaissance and the often contrived spaces of the preceding Mannerist period. While Renaissance buildings usually presented an equally impressive aspect from all sides, Baroque buildings encouraged both main and secondary viewpoints.

It was not so to begin with however, and the precursors of full-blown Baroque, usually working in Rome, departed from the principles of the High Renaissance in quite a subtle manner.

Vignola & Il Gesù

One of the earliest examples came in the form of an addition to Giacomo Barozzi da Vignola's church Il Gesù. Vignola had created a longitudinal church with an exceptionally open and uncluttered layout; there was no aisle, chancel or columnar obstructions to the worshipper's simple enjoyment of the space. Vignola's long time patron Alessandro Farnese had supported this view of the interior but rejected the aging Vignola's proposal for the façade, giving the task instead to the younger Giacomo della Porta. In response della Porta made a break with tradition and created a façade of considerable complexity and sculptural force that together created a sense of occasion for the approaching worshipper. Unlike any classical solution it was theatrical in its effects, mainly due to the device of making the volume of the orders intensify as they drew nearer to the central entrance. Above, rich and ornate decoration reinforced the psychological impact of a building now attuned to its users' expectations rather than to its own aesthetic order.

motives & ambitions

Baroque art and architecture differed from those of the Renaissance in that their influence spread quite rapidly from Italy to Spain, Hungary, Austria and the Catholic parts of Germany. Following The Reformation a permanent rift had formed between Catholic Italy and the newly Protestant countries of Holland, most of Germany and England.

The Catholic Church, engine of architecture and art in Italy, was looking to reinforce its strength in its strongholds. The Reformation was not the only major difficulty that the church had to deal with: the Renaissance, with its Humanist emphasis on the individual and its reverence for the 'pagan' culture of ancient Rome, had not always endorsed the Church quite as emphatically as its built output might suggest. The result had been a further erosion of the church's standing.

The spirit of the 17th century was also one in which a combination of burgeoning scientific thought (by definition inimical to religious belief) and the growth of secular power bases throughout Europe further threatened the traditional power of religion in general, and of the Roman Catholic Church in particular.

There was then an understandable inclination for the Church to return with renewed vigour to its traditional practice of deploying the tools of painting, sculpture and architecture to inspire worshippers to seek spiritual renewal. Now it would also encourage a style of potent theatrical presentation so alluring that it risked erring on the side of overblown ornateness and overwrought gestures.

The Reformation

The late medieval Catholic Church, particularly in the office of the papacy, was deeply involved in the political life of western Europe. Intrigues and political skullduggery, in combination with the church's great power and wealth, debilitated the church as a spiritual force. Abuses and corruption were widespread. The Reformation was a 16th century religious and political reaction against this, a bid to reform the Roman Catholic Church in Europe. The reformers' discontent was finally galvanised by a German priest Martin Luther in 1517 and the effects were far-reaching, leading as they did to the establishment of Protestant churches. The Reformation was endorsed when the absolute monarchies gave it support by challenging the power of the papacy, and confiscating church wealth.

below The huge altar piece in Bernini's church of Sant' Andrea al Quirinale in Rome

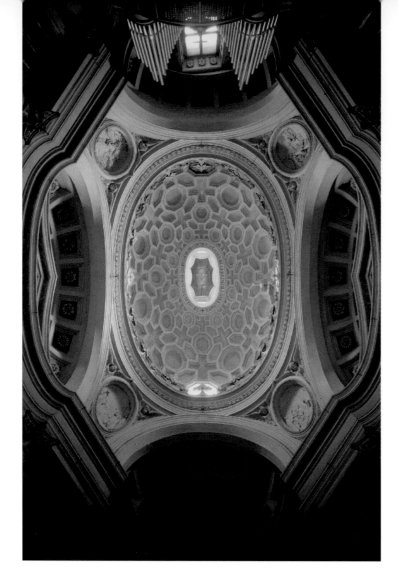

left The domed ceiling of San Carlo alle Quattro Fontane, the first masterwork of Francesco Borromini

Carlo Maderno 1556–1629

Maderno began his architectural career in Rome and the success of his first major commission, the façade of Santa Susanna, built between 1597 and 1603.

This façade was clearly much influenced by della Porta's façade for Il Gesù which it effectively exaggerates in an entirely positive way. The Santa Susanna facade, partly because it is taller and narrower, is even more dramatic in its invitational approach, and now the cool control of the Renaissance has entirely given way to powerful decorative features all aimed at preparing the visitor for a theatrical religious experience.

The success of this façade led to Maderno's being appointed, in 1603, as the chief architect to the building that seems to have exercised more architectural talent over a longer period of time than any other: Saint Peter's, Rome, at this point still unfinished even after a century.

Maderno designed the nave and a new façade for Saint Peter's where in adding a traditional nave, so he reverted to the scheme of early Christian and medieval cathedrals and abandoned Michelangelo's Greek-cross plan.

He next took the façade design, which hd been inaugurated by della Porta and refined by himself at Santa Susanna, to a new and adventurous level. Starting with a pedimented columnar porch (the classic Renaissance-style temple front) he went on to accentuate the large scale architectural effects that lead up to it by increasing the volume and rhythm of the enormous membering at each interval.

Despite a serious drawback caused by the now lengthened nave – namely that the new façade now obscures much of the dome – this was certainly a bold and successful departure. Maderno's plan was carried out between 1607 and 1615 and firmly established once and for all the Baroque principles of innovation, movement and drama in a major building.

Francesco Borromini 1599–1667

Borromini, another definitive practitioner of the Italian Baroque style, made his name with the church of S. Carlo alle Quattro Fontane, Rome, a building which serves to illustrate the primary concerns of a long and productive career.

The interior was of oval design with complex and unexpected effects, including undulating walls of stone that appeared as almost pliable planes richly decorated with cornices, mouldings, pediments and deep entablature. The result was a sense of dynamism, of active space directly opposed to preceding traditions of stability and control.

Due to funding problems, Borromini only returned to create the façade of S. Carlo alle Quattro Fontane some 20 years later, towards the end of his career. It was to be another radical showpiece, a rhythmic, curvilinear solution that echoed the interior and took new freedom with the orders, treating them like sculptural forms rather than icons.

In the context of urban development, Borromini did produce some unbuilt schemes that seem to suggest that his sensibilities were well attuned to town planning considerations too, revealing a keen awareness of the importance of the relationship between his buildings to the surrounding fabric. When he was planning a setting for the façade of S. Giovanni in Laterano by developing a piazza, he prescribed that a street passing through it should be surrounded by 24 uniform building fronts dedicated to creating a uniform feeling of enclosed space.

Pietro da Cortona 1596–1669

Pietro da Cortona was the fourth great exponent of Baroque style, a favourite of Pope Alexander VII and a man whose fame as an architect (he was yet another multi-disciplinary talent) reached its zenith in the 1630s with the design of the Church of SS. Luca e Martina, Rome, and his ceiling fresco *Allegory of Divine Providence* created for the Barberini Palace there.

SS. Luca e Martina marks a further departure in Baroque architecture away from the styles of either Bernini or Borromini with both its swelling interior walls and the powerfully articulated façade.

His façade for the church of Santa Maria della Pace was part of Pope Alexander's modernisation scheme for Rome, and had been in fact originally designed for another more obscurely-sited Roman church. It is another bold design, this time using four pairs of Tuscan columns in an arrangement that recalls Bramante's Tempietto. However the façade gains added interest from the modifications which were made to the surrounding city fabric which include a new piazza and an adaptation of the surrounding houses that effectively turns them into lateral articulated wings to the church façade.

Gianlorenzo Bernini 1598–1680

The greatest sculptor of the 17th century was also an outstanding architect. Protégé of Pope Urban VIII, his first architectural work was the remodeled Church of Santa Bibiana in Rome. Bernini was also commissioned to build a symbolic structure over the tomb of St. Peter in St. Peter's Basilica. He created a huge gilt-bronze baldachin with twisted columns and an upper framework flanked by four angels to support an orb and cross. As tall as a four-storey building, the baldachin is a startling blend of sculpture, architecture and stage design, and is without doubt the first unequivocal Baroque monument and forms the anchor of a programme of interior decoration that Bernini created interior of St. Peter's.

Bernini's reputation as the definitive Baroque architect rests on his ability to create great work in which dazzling effects did not detract from a superb sense of space and architectural effect. If his St Peter's baldachin was great theatre, then the Cornaro Chapel he designed in St Maria della Vittoria must count as grand opera. Above the altar of the shallow chapel Bernini created an oval niche crowned by a curved, broken pediment and framed by columns carefully positioned to improve sightlines. This niche provides a stage upon which

Bernini shows Saint Theresa about to be impaled by an arrow of divine love – a highly expressive tableau which includes a carved audience seated in carved theatre boxes on the lateral walls of the chapel. This audience represents members of the Cornaro family. Everywhere rich effects predominate, a painted heaven, artificial rays of celestial light augmented by real ones from a strategically placed window, and swirling stucco clouds. *The Ecstasy of St. Teresa* is no sculpture in any conventional sense. It is a theatrical event made up of sculpture, painting, and light, consciously designed to draw the churchgoer into the mood of a religious experience.

Increasingly Bernini sought to control the environments of his statuary and this led him to execute more architecture. Accordingly his Church of Sant'Andrea al Quirinale, Rome, featured a dramatic high altar, a dome soaring heavenward, and an unconventional oval plan.

However Bernini's major architectural achievement returns us yet again to St. Peter's Basilica which he complemented with a scheme so dramatic as to give the building its defining external image from this point on. His colonnade enclosing the piazza was designed to hold the crowd assembled for papal benedictions. It was a scheme that

in a previous age might have been achieved with simple practicality or sombre grandeur. In Bernini's hands it became another huge piece of theatre: an inspired counterbalance to the broad façade of St. Peter's itself; a mighty oval attached to the church by a trapezoidal forecourt; a blatant but superbly-proportioned image of the enfolding arms of the mother church.

Its freestanding colonnades were a particularly clever solution to the need for an enclosure that was not a barrier, and everything about the piazza leads and encourages the visitor inwards to the church: it is a summation of those early Baroque church façades and the epitome of the church's ambitions for Baroque architecture as a whole.

below The collonade enclosing the piazza in front of St. Peter's Basilica in the Vatican, Rome

Baldachin

A baldachin is a decorative canopy over an altar or tomb. It is usually a freestanding structure supported on columns. The word derives from the Spanish *baldaquin,* an Eastern brocade traditionally used as a canopy over an altar or doorway.

Johann Fischer von Erlach
1656–1723

Fischer, an Austrian sculptor and architect developed an idiosyncratic Baroque style who had as a young man entered the workshop of Bernini, later published a comparative study of architecture (*Entwurf einer historischen Architektur*) and produced at least one great building, the Karlskirche (Church of St. Charles Borromeo) which he began in 1715.

Charles VI commissioned the Karlskirche (left) as an offering to his patron saint for the city's deliverance from an epidemic of the plague but the building Fischer delivered was not just a monument, it was an ambitious codification of elements from the great religious buildings of all time. The architectural historian in Fischer sought to blend elements of everything from St. Peter's in Rome, and the Hagia Sophia in Istanbul with St. Paul's Cathedral and the Dôme des Invalides. This bizarre ambition produced a complex but improbably successful building in which the life of St. Charles is glorified on a pair of triumphal columns flanking the portico. Fischer died before the building was fully completed although his son, Joseph Emanuel Fischer von Erlach, completed it with only minor amendments.

karlskirche, vienna

out of italy

Baroque proved an eminently exportable style, particularly in its late form, often referred to as Rococo, particularly in its later form as adopted – and largely defined – by the French.

Rococo was a style not only in architecture but also in decorative arts, painting and sculpture identified by a lighter decorative feel than Baroque and an unrestrained use of stylised forms of nature in ornamentation. The word derives from the French word *rocaille* describing the shell-covered rockwork that was once used to decorate artificial grottoes.

France

France not only embraced the late Baroque, but it made a lasting impression upon the style with Louis XIV's Palace of Versailles and its spectacular garden setting. Here was the Baroque ideal given unrestrained freedom and an apparently limitless budget. Versailles was intended to be a visible expression of the glory of France, and of its king, at the time Europe's most powerful ruler. Its immensely ambitious layout and gardens were matched by interiors of almost unimaginable sumptuousness, an explosion of illusory art, fanciful stucco, marble, bronze and sold silver.

Versailles' ornate splendour demonstrated more clearly than ever before or since what could happen when an ornate religiously-inspired style was adapted to glorify royalty and the state.

Germany & Austria

German and Austrian architects who had studied in Rome became the standard bearers of Baroque expansion at home.

Fischer von Erlach and Hildebrandt were the leading names in Austria, the Asam Brothers and Balthasar Neumann in Bavaria.

Balthasar Neumann 1687–1753

No discussion of Baroque is complete without mention of one of Europe's greatest palaces, The Würzburg Rezidenz.

Although it had originally been proposed by two amateur architects, it was not until 1737, when Neumann's astonishingly ambitious staircase was designed and built, that the Rezidenz began to take shape and Neumann took over other aspects of the palace. Above the staircase a near miraculous ceiling floats on a single vault, an unexpectedly large space that would later be decorated by Tiepolo. Neumann also changed the original location of an associated chapel, repositioning it so that it might rise to the full height of the palace and, in doing so, enabled the creation of an interior of great richness with intersecting vaults placed over a ground plan of overlapping ellipses.

Work on the Residenz continued at intervals after Neumann's death in 1753.

Johann Lucas von Hildebrandt 1668–1745

Born, despite his name, in Genoa, Hildebrandt studied in the studio of Fontana in Rome before moving to Vienna. He was a military engineer as well as an architect and among his many works two of the most outstanding are the Belvedere in Vienna, summer residence of Prince Eugene of Savoy 1700–23, and the Episcopal residence at Würzburg, Germany, 1729–37.

Hildebrandt was much influenced by Italian late-Baroque style and became famous for his use of almost pictorial motifs and effects realised in purely architectural terms.

right The chapel in the Rezidenz in Würzburg, Germany, designed by Balthasar Neumann

The Church of Sankt Johannes Nepomuk

The Church of Sankt Johannes Nepomuk at Munich (1733–46), in a rare tribute, is equally well known to the world as the Asamkirche, in honour of its two architects.

The Asam brothers' masterpiece it is a dizzying achievement in the Bavarian High Baroque style. The Asams were the decorators as well as the architects of this small church. Its tall, narrow interior, ethereally lit from above, has two levels separated by a gallery that progresses sinuously along the wall.

Virtually an architectural encyclopaedia of quotations from the Italian Baroque masters, the awesome interior is richly decorated with paint, stucco work, sculpture and gilt. The ceiling is decorated with painted figures rising into a space that seems almost to leave the physical limits of the church building.

Somewhat unexpectedly it is here in Munich, endistanced in more senses than one from the Roman source of Baroque, that the style's two extremes are most successfully combined. Here is the architectural clarity of expression inaugurated by Borromini, but here too is a level of theatricality worthy of Bernini.

Here, not for the first time we can see the principles of a style most compactly and clearly expressed in an exported form through the work of foreign admirers and exponents.

Cosmas and Egid Asam
1686–1739, 1692–1750

The Asam brothers were part of a generation of Germans educated in Rome in the Italian Baroque tradition as part of a concerted move to replace itinerant Italian artists with the home-grown product. Their buildings contain sometimes startling levels of dramatic intensity. Cosmas Asam had studied in Rome with Pierleone Ghezzi from 1712 to 1714 and brothers' first religious commissions revealed their interest in Bernini's concept of theatrical religious set pieces where all the decorative elements combined to involve the spectator in the drama.

Throughout their work their respective contributions of decorative and architectural elements were hard to separate either in terms of authorship or effect. Their undoubted masterpiece is the extraordinary The Church of Sankt Johannes Nepomuk in Munich. Their other major works, which confirm them as supreme masters of High Baroque or Rococo style include the cloister church in the Benedictine abbey of Weltenburg which contains their gilded sculpture *St. George and the Dragon*, and the Ursuline church at Straubing.

below The narrow façade of the Church of Sankt Johannes Nepomuk in Munich, fronting unexpected baroque treasures within

right The amazing interior of the 'Asamkirche' (Sankt Johannes Nepomuk) by the brothers Asam

asamkirche, munich

England

Even in England, inimical in spirit and climate to Italian Baroque, there was a keen interest in some of its architectural effects, not least the curvilinear forms of Bernini. A notable if isolated example is the Cathedral of St. Philip, Birmingham (1710), by Thomas Archer. In general though it was the leading architectural thinkers who adapted the broader strands of the Baroque. Sir James Gibbs managed to blend both Baroque and Palladian thinking in a number of buildings, the best-known of which is his 1720 St. Martin-in-the-Fields, facing London's Trafalgar Square, where a classical temple front was improbably matched with a tall steeple. St. Martin's nonetheless was to set the pattern for countless other English churches.

Inigo Jones 1573–1652

It may seem odd that Inigo Jones, heavily influenced as he was by Palladio, should have been drawn to the increasingly decorative and effusive Baroque style at all. He was, though, attracted by its spirit at least and sought to incorporate it into in his own late works. In his Queen's Chapel of 1623 and Whitehall Palace of 1638 he brought to London something of the spirit of northern Italy if in a rather modulated and controlled form.

Sir Christopher Wren 1632–1723

Wren also gentrified English Baroque for an English audience. His St. Stephen's, Walbrook, London (1672), recalls the earlier period of Italian Baroque in its with its structural complexity and multiplicity of viewpoints. His masterpiece of St. Paul's Cathedral, London (1675–1711), also owes a debt to French and Italian examples of the Baroque period, notably the use of space which is decidedly un-English. Of Wren's larger Baroque building complexes, the Royal Hospital Greenwich, 1696, is outstanding with its impressive vista flanked by long columned colonnades leading to the domes of the chapel and the Painted Hall. Such complexes prepared the way for the epic work of Vanbrugh.

Sir John Vanbrugh 1664–1726

Vanbrugh's Castle Howard in Yorkshire, and Blenheim Palace in Oxfordshire, represent the summation of the Baroque in England. Blenheim Palace is a quite colossal palace, wildly exceeding its original purpose as a prestigious reward for the Duke of Marlborough and becoming instead a British National Monument that eclipses the impact of Buckingham Palace and most other royal buildings. Its tendency to try to be a compendium of architectural styles is confusing rather than successful, but for sheer Baroque scale of ambition it remains a remarkable monumental building by any standards.

Spain & Portugal

Spain too managed to take various aspects of Baroque and Rococo architecture whilst modifying it to local preferences. In Spain there was generally a greater emphasis put on surface decoration than on deep-etched details.

This localising approach is well demonstrated in two facades: that of the Granada cathedral (1667) by Alonso Cano, and that of Jaén (1667), by Eufrasio López de Rojas. In both cases there is evidence of the influence of local craft traditions.

José Benito Churriguera favoured rich ornamentation to such an extent that 'Churrigueresque' became a label for late 17th century and early 18th century Spanish architecture. Among the most famous of the Churrigueresque masters was Pedro di Ribera who designed a memorable portal for the Hospice of San Fernando in 1722.

This conformed to the original model of late Baroque in its sinuous lines, but to this introduced encrusted surface decorations of such density and florid excess that the result is inevitably redolent of the etymological origins of Rococo: rocaille, the decorative shell-covered rockwork used to decorate artificial grottoes.

Late Baroque in Spain is well represented by the Chapel of Our Lady of Pilar in the cathedral of Saragossa (1750), by Ventura Rodríguez, who, demonstrated himself to be the supreme master of the fully developed High Baroque/Rococo in its modified Spanish form.

Portuguese Baroque building was fuelled by wealth from the gold and diamond mines of Brazil. Celebration of new national wealth was ideally suited to the opulent style although the buildings were as often as not designed by foreigners. The Royal Library of the University of Coimbra built between 1716 and 1728, is a probable exception being ascribed to a local architect, Gaspar Ferreira.

Portugal's local preference was for worship to incorporate as far as possible something of the feel of pleasure pavilions and of outdoor recreational spaces. It is in this spirit that the extraordinary and very appealing pilgrimage church of Bom Jesus do Monte appears on a hilltop in Northern Portugal, by Cruz Amarante.

From the first cautious explorations of theatrical effect in church façades to the wilder decorative set pieces that marked its culmination, Baroque was always an adventure – albeit often over-the-top – in style. As a political phenomenon it was limited in purpose to reinforcing the by-then ebbing power of the church; as a means of expression it was, in the end, as much about glorification of the architect as anything else; in all other respects it was as irrelevant to the development of the city form as any élite form must be.

Even so, every major architectural development makes its own contribution to the cumulative mix of ideas, and Baroque certainly provided some of architecture's most dazzling examples. Born out of reaction to the past rather than aspiration for the future, it was relatively short-lived, and soon a much more pressing period of social upheaval would return architecture to reality on the ground rather than elaborately decorated pie in the sky.

left Wren's masterpiece in the middle of the City of London, St. Paul's Cathedral

below The incredible maze-like entrance steps by Cruz Amarante leading to the Bom Jesus do Monte church in Braga, Northern Portugal

8

into the first
industrial age

08

from style to structure

The stylistic progressions of the Renaissance and the Baroque finally ran their course and were gradually replaced with a European-wide spirit of sobriety in building design.

There were a number of historical reasons for this, the most significant of which would be the French Revolution of 1789 which reminded everyone else of the fragility of political power. If the French monarchy could be overturned, so could any state. This sombre realisation was not one likely to encourage more architectural *fol de rols* and stylistic adventures like the Palace of Versailles; instead it would promote a new gravitas in building design.

Another reason was that Baroque had only ever really flourished in Catholic countries, and with the balance of power moving away from Rome and towards the Protestant regions of Europe, a widespread reaction against Baroque and Rococo was inevitable.

Finally there was a social enthusiasm – a new craze for archaeology, often pursued in a very dilettante fashion, but no less enthusiastically for that. Greek ruins were suddenly *de rigueur* as The Grand Tour to the sites of antiquity became a fashionable part of the education of the young gentlemen of Europe.

Surrounding this rediscovery of Greece was a whole industry of publications, engravings and paintings echoing the flurry of activity that had accompanied the onset of The Renaissance itself.

One of these was an essay by a French Jesuit, Abbé Marc-Antoine Laugier, whose *Essai sur l'architecture* was published in French in 1753 and in English two years later.

Recommending a return to rationalism and simplicity, and taking the primitive hut as his model of the basic expression of human needs, Laugier rejected the excesses of the Baroque/Rococo period arguing that all forms having no structural or functional purpose should be abandoned. Nothing could have been further from the spirit of recent grand architecture and by the middle of the 18th century, the days of Baroque and Rococo architecture were numbered.

Laugier was no building designer but his published opinions certainly caught the spirit of the times and his theories were adopted by a self-taught architect Jacques Germain Soufflot. In 1755 Jacques Soufflot began designing the church of Sainte-Geneviève, which was planned to be the principal church of Paris – an ambition which was soon doomed to be derailed by the Revolution.

The building plan was essentially a Greek cross, and the façade a large temple front. A dome based on that of St Paul's was supported exclusively on pillars connected by straight entablatures plus four triangular piers at the corners. (This arrangement proved inadequate eventually and buttresses had to be used). Ironically the building's classical leanings meant that when the Revolution abolished religion, the church was easily de-sanctified and rechristened the Panthéon.

Thus began another Classical age, often dubbed the Neoclassical period so as to distinguish it from the original architectural influences upon which it was based.

Building Technology: a reprise

Depending on their location, mankind's earliest shelters were built from foliage, animal skins, stones, ice or mud. Gradually wood and stone came to predominate as the materials best suited to permanent structures. Where wood was plentiful it was split into planks and then cut into posts which were used to support roofs and to subdivide the space into sections or rooms.

Stone construction began three or four thousand years before the birth of Christ. The ancient Greeks built with pieces of stone that were very skilfully dressed and then fitted together dry, although occasionally clay and later mortar were used. Concrete followed, thanks to the Romans, and eventually bricks made from clay made possible the building of the arches, vaults, and domes.

The above summary takes us to late Roman times, after which technological change had been slower, incremental and never a process that initiated radical change. In the mid-18th century, at the time of Marc-Antoine Laugier's ruminations on building essentials, it must have seemed that building technology had gone as far as it was ever going, that the whole range of opportunities had now been tried and it was time to get back to basics.

Neoclassicism

Neoclassicism has been the subject of many studies and varying interpretations. Its austere beginnings were often compromised by a streak of romanticism. It spread throughout Europe but was particularly strong in England where it had significant impact on the layouts of at least two cities, Bath and London, with John Wood the Younger's Royal Crescent and John Nash's terraces around Regent's Park. For the main part though, a building style was a gestural approach to specific major building types, not a rational approach to the development of the city. The style even spread to the colonies, with exuberant Neoclassical experiments being tried from Virginia to Philadelphia. A detailed consideration of the style is beyond the scope of this book, but it is an essential prologue to the next major development which was to return the design of cities, not just buildings, to centre stage, even as it changed the world forever.

By the start of the 19th century the placatory effect of a return to classical values in the arts and architecture had disappeared. Quite apart from the diversions that made Neoclassicism more of a playful style than supporters of Laugier might have hoped, the spirit of the age was increasingly out of sympathy with more replaying of old orders of things.

The impact of the French Revolution was unprecedented. It had enfranchised the middle classes who were becoming a force to be reckoned with all over Europe. It was they, not the patrician class, who were becoming the arbiters of taste. The Revolution that had sought to free the workers had actually empowered the bourgeoisie, and if that were not enough to send shivers down the spines of the traditional masters, another revolution was underway whose effects would never disappear.

above   A fine example of Neoclassicism in Paris, the Comedie Française

coalbrookdale bridge, shropshire

Iron

Iron was the structural material that triggered the process although it had already been used in construction hundreds of years before the first industrial age. Iron chain suspension bridges were known to have existed in 15th century China. Even the tension chains in the dome of St. Peter's were of iron. Now, though, for the first time iron was being produced on a large-scale and inexpensive basis, mainly due to the innovative work of Abraham Darby, who in 1709 for the first time used coke as a fuel for smelting.

In 1800 world production of iron was 825,000 tons. By 1830 it was 1,825,000 tons. By 1900 it had reached almost 40,000,000 tons. With iron much more readily available, machinery could be built relatively easily, so accelerating the development of radical new inventions that would have significant ramifications of their own, inventions such as James Watt's double-acting steam engine of 1769.

Standard iron building elements soon appeared, pointing the way to the further development of metal buildings. However the first large cast-iron structure of the industrial age was not a building, but a bridge.

the first industrial age is born

The last half of the 18th century saw the gradual development of a series of events, mainly in Britain, that history would later come to dub the First Industrial Revolution. It began with the exploitation of natural phenomena – water and coal – and soon turned into a wave of interdependent industrial activities that spread like wildfire and changed not only building technology but also the very fabric of society.

Coalbrookdale Bridge

The bridge occupies a special place in any history of architecture. Bridge design represents an easy-to-understand reduction of architectural principles, of which the most important (and least frequently stated) is that the structure must not fall down. When it comes to bridges, unnecessary weight and overblown design gestures are usually counterproductive, so throughout history bridges have provided many effortless examples of form following function – that is to say they look the way they do because their shape was determined primarily by physical necessity, not whim

The Industrial Revolution meant that wood and stone – and their associated craft traditions – were increasingly and understandably displaced by the availability of cheaper and stronger iron.

The first exclusively iron bridge was designed by Thomas Pritchard and built by Abraham Darby in 1779. It spanned the River Severn near Coalbrookdale in England. Known variously as the Coalbrookdale Bridge, Iron Bridge or Ironbridge, the structure was actually pre-dated in construction by a French iron bridge but this was never erected. Built of cast-iron sections, the Coalbrookdale Bridge forms a ribbed arch with a 30 metre span. Interestingly it mimics the principle of compression used in stone bridges, deploying the inherent strength of cast iron in much the same way. This notion of new technology copying old is one that recurs throughout history, early motor cars being literally horseless carriages because there was nothing else for them to look like to begin with. However, less than 15 years after its construction the Coalbrookdale Bridge was to prove itself much more than a new-fangled copy of an old model when floods in the Severn region destroyed all the traditional bridges while the cast iron newcomer survived. Its reduced surfaces allowed the floodwater to pass through, when the wide, flat surfaces of the neighbouring stone bridge took the full force of the tide.

The proven success of the Coalbrookdale Bridge was duly noted by Thomas Telford, who was soon to bring considerable technical sophistication to bridge building and help establish the engineer as the first architectural heir of the Industrial Revolution.

With iron now an apparently infinitely adaptable material, the architects of the newly-industrialised mid-19th century were faced with something of a problem. What style was going to offer an appropriate response to the new freely available material?

They were not helped in their quandary by a sometimes lamentable lack of structural knowledge about the wonder material. Iron was being tested by the empirical method, hastily pressed into service for everything

Thomas Telford 1757–1834

Telford was a self-taught architect who first worked as a surveyor of public works. In this capacity he oversaw the construction of various buildings and bridges in Shropshire, England. In 1793 he was appointed as an engineer to the Ellesmere Canal Company and in this capacity built aqueducts, carrying the Ellesmere canal across two Welsh valleys. These aqueducts made innovative use of troughs made of cast-iron plates that were inserted into the masonry.

These projects established Telford's reputation and he went on to other major engineering works all over Britain including the Caledonian Canal and harbour works at Aberdeen and Dundee.

In the course of improving the roads from two English towns to the Welsh port of Holyhead, he built his two world-famous suspension bridges: one over the River Conwy and the even more ambitious Menai Straits Bridge.

More bridges and roads followed as well as tunnels and a series of canals, waterways which suddenly needed to be upgraded to meet the challenge of Britain's expanding railway system.

Telford also built the Göta Canal in Sweden and the St. Katharine Docks complex in London.

His career marks the emergence of the civil engineer as architect-designer and epitomises the spirit of a time when great engineering projects assumed heroic impact not by the application of fanciful style, but through breadth of vision and tireless effort.

far left The historic Iron Bridge at Coalbrookdale, magnificently spanning the River Severn in rural Shropshire, England

from bridges and museums to conservatories and libraries. Cast iron was the preferred form – until a spate of fires proved its vulnerability and steel replaced it in the later buildings of the century.

The steel skeleton began to emerge as a viable form although it was used with varying success, at least until a system was developed for calculating stresses accurately.

The system was complex and created, overnight, a new profession: the civil engineer. In what some may see as an early indicator of a trend, the traditional expertise of the architect was eroded by men trained for other purposes – usually in the mechanics of warfare – who were capable not only of understanding the structural behaviour of the new materials, but in some cases of thinking creatively and imaginatively about them.

Experiments With Iron

The age of experiment with iron explored various possibilities. The material so clearly expressed in bridges was introduced into British buildings of the First Industrial Age variously hidden, decorated and blatant about itself. A flour mill at Ditherington, Shropshire (1796–97) used a mix of iron beams and brick to bear the load. A cloth mill at King's Stanley, Gloucestershire (1812–13) offered a more recognisable example of an iron frame structure, self-supporting and clad in red brick. These industrial buildings clearly reflected a business-like approach to materials, where strength, fireproofing and construction cost were the criteria, not grand statements.

Elsewhere cast iron was being tentatively introduced into major public buildings. Often these were conceived in the Neoclassical or Gothic Revival

styles and their architects were unsure about how obvious they should be about admitting to new structural materials.

The British Museum (1823–46) conceals its cast-iron beams, but Buckingham Palace (1825–30) built by Nash, displayed its cast-iron Doric columns unashamedly.

In general buildings of the early industrial age tackled the problem of how to use iron in one of three ways.

They used it to manufacture already familiar forms that had originally developed out of quite different materials; they used it to modify existing forms, changing them to take advantage of iron's different physical properties; or they used it to create new forms altogether.

The completely independent iron frame without masonry adjuncts emerged slowly in a series of special building types.

The first modest example was Hungerford Fish Market of 1835 in London where timber was forbidden because of sanitation regulations. The cast-iron beams spanned 9.7 metres with 3-metre cantilevers on either side, and the hollow cast-iron columns also served as roof drains. All lateral stability was provided by the rigid joints between columns and beams.

The next type to use the full iron frame was the greenhouse, which provided a controlled luminous and thermal environment for tropical plants in the cold climate of northern Europe. Iron was often combined with glass in the construction of one of the quintessential building types of the period: the grand conservatory. The conservatory (1827–30) at Syon House, Middletsex, by Charles Fowler, and the Palm House (1845–47) at Kew Gardens, Surrey, by Decimus Burton are outstanding examples.

Brick

Brick production was industrialized in the 19th century. The simplest mechanical process imaginable – extruded mix forced through a rectangular die and sliced by a wire into unit forms – replaced the labour-intensive tradition of hand-moulding, which had been the only means of production for 3,000 years.
A continuous tunnel kiln where the bricks were moved slowly along on a conveyor belt, appeared by the end of the century. Here was a microcosm of the Industrial Revolution: bricks were now more regular, better controlled in production, cheaper and more plentifully available. Brick became one of the key building materials of the new age.

Telford's St Katharine Docks in London was an example of a well-organised new industrial environment in which iron was incorporated in to familiar building forms rather more effortlessly than was often the case in more self-important buildings.

In Britain the new Houses of Parliament represented an early challenge to architectural thought at the dawn of the age of iron. Something recalling Britain's finest hour was commissioned, and this presumed something Gothic in appearance. The architect Charles Barry recruited Augustus Pugin, an authority on Gothic, to assist and the result was a Classical style buildings with Gothic overtones. Oddly perhaps, when you look at the Houses of Parliament, Pugin and many other architects of the time, championed unadorned functionality in buildings. Nothing that did not serve a structural purpose – or at least a purpose of convenience for the user – should be included. Ironically this was a theory entirely in tune with the industrialisation of building that was already going on but which Pugin and his like affected to loathe.

Certainly there was little visual link between the grandeur of Gothic revisited and the spare skeletons of new iron skeleton buildings at their most functional, despite the prosaic fact that the bronze window frames for The Houses of Parliament were mass-produced in Birmingham. However the spirit was the same and the lessons for the future of architecture inexorable. From now on fundamental issues of form and function would be polarised in a way never seen before.

far left The iron-framed Hungerford Fish Market in London

above The Palm House, built between 1845 and 1847 at Kew Gardens in Surrey, England

Social Changes

Changes in the city and town life brought about by the First Industrial Age were to begin with more social than organisational. Suddenly the concept of urban leisure appeared. Although the main beneficiaries of the changing social order were middle class, gradually the working class too began to see its role redefined.

As factory work replaced traditional manufacturing, the habits of mass production meant that workers, in a limited way, now had time and money for leisure pursuits. So great was the novelty of a system that provided any free time at all that some workers would sometimes simply not go to work if they could afford it: free time was preferable to higher earnings.

The result was an explosion of crude but popular street entertainments which were frowned upon by the authorities as a potential threat to public order. The urban police forces established at the start of the 19th century to combat crime, found themselves increasingly occupied with the effects of entertainment-related incidents and affrays.

Drinking together became a recreational outlet for men, creating its own social environment in the bars that appeared in working-class sections of most towns. The patterns of traditional leisure were changing almost as fast as the patterns of traditional labour had done. Local festivals and community-based entertainments gave way to spectator events – circuses or concerts, where large crowds paid an admission charge for professional entertainers to divert them.

Inevitably cities started to grow in size as the engines of industry fired up. The effect on family life was considerable both for the bourgeoisie and the working classes. Work, and the family patterns it had set, moved away from home and home was never the same again. Entrepreneurs who blithely assumed that their wives would help them set up business on the grounds that wives had always helped with the work, soon discovered that such values could not be transferred from one era to another. Soon the fashionable homes that a successful business generated started to be located in districts away from the town's commercial area, and therefore demanded a whole new management regime of their own. Family men became breadwinners and their wives became the domestic specialists.

A New Need For Buildings

The 19th century was a boom period for architects and other building specialists, notably the civil engineer. Not only was there new prosperity brought about by industrial change, the changing order of things was altering the needs of towns and cities, bringing about a requirement for new types of buildings.

The newly rich were in need of country houses, as the newly rich usually are. At the other end of the spectrum, city churches were needed for the newly poor who had been created by the sudden shift in working practices from home unit to mass production. New leisure, new commerce and a new sense of civic pride were also demanding appropriate buildings.

In Britain these might take the form of a grand new town hall like that of Leeds, built in 1853 as the result of a competition won by Cuthbert Brodrick. The fact that Brodrick was young and relatively unknown, stands in marked contrast to the Establishment spirit in which Barry and Pugin were appointed to design the Houses of Parliament. Even so he created a building that was to become an icon of civic pride in the *nouveau riche* industrial city. With its massive Corinthian order and Baroque tower and dome, Leeds Town Hall was no literal expression of the new technology, but it could be said to share its vigour and optimism.

This unresolved tension between traditional elements of Classicism and the expressive possibilities of the rapidly emerging new technologies made for some uneasy alliances and extreme opinions. When Benjamin Baker built the Forth Bridge at the end of the century it outraged many. This staggering structure with its three mighty cantilevered elements, would be denounced by William Morris as the apogee of bad taste: 'every improvement in machinery was uglier and uglier until they reached the supremest specimen of all ugliness, the Forth Bridge'.

Bibliothèque Ste.-Geneviève

In France at least one quite outstanding building demonstrated how the new technology might be incorporated effortlessly into a fine piece of architecture. The Bibliothèque Ste.-Geneviève in Paris, built between 1842 and 1850 by Henri Labrouste, was something of a leap of faith into new construction materials.

There was no real need to use iron elements at all inside this simple rectangular two-storey masonry shell. A reading room fills the upper storey, above various stacking and storage areas, and it is a ferrous structure of considerable elegance, with a slender central row of cast-iron Doric columns dividing the interior into two aisles and supporting open ironwork arches that in turn support reinforced plaster barrel arches. The whole thing is so gracefully arranged and seems so evocative of abstract influences that it comes as something of a shock to realise that Labrouste's intention was to make the building look like a book.

Simple mimicry was out of the question, but the internal geometry and some 800 inscriptions of authors' names, as well as a number of other subtle devices make his intentions clear.

As the deceptively simple building gradually reveals itself as being actually more complex, it becomes obvious that Labrouste used cast-iron in an entirely considered way as part of his plan, not just as a gesture in favour of the new or in defence of the old.

left The familiar Neoclassicism of the British Houses of Parliament

below The interior of the Bibliothèque (Library) Ste. Geneviève, Paris, with the arches inspired by the rounded binding of books

Cement

Cement, we know, was no new invention. In use since Roman times it remained unchanged until 1824 when Joseph Aspdin patented the first true artificial cement, which he called Portland Cement, a name intended to imply that it was of the same superior quality as Portland stone. Aspdin burned limestone and clay together in a kiln the clay providing silicon compounds that, when water was added, formed stronger bonds than the calcium compounds of limestone. However even in its new improved form, cement's poor tensile strength limited its applications until iron and steel came into widespread use. Then the cheapest form of iron – long thin bars – which had enormous tensile strength, could be embedded in concrete to make ferro-concrete. Beams, columns, arches, vaults and walls of new slimmer dimensions were suddenly possible.

right   A derelict Albert Dock before its refurbishment in the 1980s

below   The Albert Dock revived as (amongst other things) the site of the Merseyside Maritime Museum

far right   The imposing collonades of the Dock with the Liver Building visible in the background

albert dock

Albert Dock

The Albert Dock in Liverpool is neither a world-famous arrangement of buildings nor an unusually innovative example of the use of new technology. However it remains of exceptional interest for several reasons.

In the first place it was, to begin with, simply a dock. No mighty monument to personality, religion or state, it served a functional 19th century purpose in a vigorous industrial northern city.

Perhaps for this reason it combined traditional and new materials in a particularly unselfconscious way. The industries serving the building trade – having been kick-started in many cases by the demands of the century's great civil engineering projects – had begun to produce a wide range of artefacts in iron that increased the options open to architects.

The architect of Albert Dock was Jesse Hartley who created a truly vast warehouse scheme occupying no less than seven acres next to the River Mersey. Hartley's buildings were iron-framed, clad in brick and supported on massive cast-iron Doric columns. They were designed simply for their straightforward functional purpose: to store and transfer goods – spices, sugar and other commodities.

Albert Dock represents a comprehensive sum of parts: the very latest type of building framework; a copious use of the newly mass-produced brick to disguise that framework; and a bold reinterpretation of the classical column, reinvented in a highly visible use of a material that owed nothing to ancient Greece and everything to Victorian technology. All that was missing were the old-fashioned lofty ideals of a building as expression of some religious or secular ideal. Even so the dock was opened by royalty – in 1845 by the eponymous Prince Albert – and in a sense it clearly was a monument as well as a practical working complex. It celebrated a new age of muscular energy and grand scale enterprise.

When Albert Dock was in its heyday, it was no less than a small industrial town with its own internal logic and rhythm of activities. When Liverpool declined in the second half of the 20th century Albert Dock in ruins provided a suitably bleak image of a now derelict industrial past. Finally, and a good reason for choosing it as an exemplar of the First Industrial Age, Albert Dock enjoyed an improbable renaissance of its own in the 1980s when it became one of those decaying urban areas in Britain to qualify for redevelopment for leisure purposes. When in addition to being the new home of shops, restaurants, apartments and television studio facilities it was also chosen as the site of an extension to London's Tate Gallery, designed by James Stirling, Albert Dock came full circle. People now admired its architecture for all those symbolic values about the past that it now seemed to possess: monumentality, self-confidence, structural soundness. An estimable contemporary architect had converted storage space for commodities into display spaces for 20th century art. Paintings by Rothko hung where sugar had been warehoused, and if the interior supporting columns were not ideal for an art gallery, the gentrification exercise remained a curiously worthwhile one. Albert Dock was one of the first responses to Victorian prosperity and the new iron age, a building of its time with no aspirations to being inspirational. This practicality of purpose did not, in the end, prevent it from becoming inspirational after all.

timber iron & steel in the USA

Timber

The vast forests of North America meant that the coming of the industrial age took a particular turn that was to have a lasting impact on the built environment. Large forests of pine and softwood fir could now effectively be 'processed' by water-powered sawmills. Standard units of timber were being produced in large quantities by the early part of the 19th century, however it was the advent of inexpensive nails in the 1830s that triggered a significant innovation in building construction: the balloon frame.

This was a cheap system of assembling timber frames for building. Walls were framed by vertical studs, placed at about 40cm intervals measured at the centre which supported the roof and floor joists and were made stable with diagonal braces or boards. The result was a general-purpose rigid box freed of heavy timbers and jointing, capable of being penetrated with doors and windows at more or less any point. Almost any sort of interior and exterior surfacing materials could be applied, including stucco or brick veneer. The balloon frame building, easily and cheaply assembled from simple standardised materials and held together with nails, remains a popular method of construction today.

Iron & Steel

In 19th century America there was little to match the amount of cast-iron building experiments taking place in Britain, although the Harper Brothers Building of 1849 by Corlies & Bogardus. Also in New York, John Kellum's design for Stewart's Department Store used a new a cast iron facing style, but in general iron was more often used to mimic stone to which it was seen as a low-maintenance alternative.

A stunning and often underrated structure, the Brooklyn Bridge, built between 1869 and 1883, was the first suspension bridge to use steel for cable wire. Although it is the skyscrapers of Chicago that are often considered to represent the start of a genuine native architecture in America, Brooklyn Bridge was the truly heroic symbol of new technology in the service of an energetic young nation. Building the bridge involved fraud, spectacular accidents and much loss of human life. Anyone studying the problems involved must marvel that it was ever built at all, let alone so magnificently. Its 485-metre main span was the longest in the world until the completion of the Firth of Forth cantilever bridge in Scotland.

The End of The Beginning

There is something of a problem inherent in looking back at a period as dynamic as the early days of the new industrial age, particularly in relation to its impact on urban spaces. In many parts of Europe the city was in turmoil, not only because of the long-felt aftermath of the French Revolution but also because of the impact of the Napoleonic Wars which, through conscription, had disrupted everyday life further even as the new social patterns of industrialisation were being set.

From the point of view of buildings there is a further difficulty in that today we have rather less difficulty admiring the 'low' end of iron

above The Brooklyn Bridge which spans New York's East River from the borough of Brooklyn to Manhattan

architecture than did a contemporary viewer who often still exclusively equated only the classical ideal with great architecture. If we now see romance, and sometimes genius, in the everyday geometries of working buildings of the 19th century – the markets, exchanges and factories – few did at the time, especially those who had to work in them. For them there was no obvious iron equivalent of the great church monuments of previous ages, no mighty cathedrals to the Industrial Revolution. Soon there would be.

In a rapidly changing world in which trade and national pride were of enormous importance, there was a pressing need to create a series of exhibition forums larger in scale than anything that had gone before. The latter half of the 19th century would therefore be the Age of The Exhibitions in which immense displays of inventions and products spanning household good, transportation, industrial machinery, applied arts and more, all displayed in an extravagant spirit of national pride and a lack of inhibition and restraint more evocative of the fairground than the chamber of commerce.

These breathtaking exhibitions would be housed in the very fabric of the new revolution, iron – but it was iron glazed and shaped into epic structures, futuristic in their day, which were designed to supply a place of worship for the masses as the First Industrial Age began inexorably to merge into the Second.

below An interior view of the dome of the Neoclassic Panthéon in Paris, based on its Roman namesake

the 19th century metropolis

9

the spirit of the century

The term Industrial Revolution is often criticised for inaccurately suggesting a sudden and abrupt change. In broad historical terms this may have been so, but in terms of daily life it was more a time of uncertainty marked by parallel or overlapping developments which at first few could claim to understand for their historical significance. To put some kind of perspective on this, here are some of the key events that, after centuries of slow, diffused and incremental technological change, occurred within a 150-year period.

In the building industry, craftsmanship had changed completely as a result of the new methods of manufacturing and mass-production. Not only the building elements but the building processes were affected. Site operations could now be mechanised, and management of these new grand sites was usually beyond the old craft-based firms. This led to the rise of the building contractor. At the same time there were new demands being made by the changed industries themselves. Quite apart from the prevailing architectural solution to factory building itself, new technical services were being specified in the form of heating, sanitation and ventilation. Domestic building quickly caught on to the advantages of such services and demanded them too.

Steam heating systems, a variation of the central heating systems not seen since the days of Ancient Rome, began to appear during the 19th century. Gas lighting came to London at the start of the century and electric lighting, – albeit initially expensive and potentially dangerous – arrived later, as did elevators, telephones and mechanical ventilation systems.

England had been the cradle of the revolution, and if no one was entirely sure what to make of it all, help was at hand. An event was staged in London in 1851 that was designed to concentrate everyone's attention on the new possibilities of architecture, transport, engineering and all the other areas of human endeavour and ingenuity that had so recently gone through radical change and made Britain not only the workshop of the world but the premier influence on the industrialization of other countries.

The Great Exhibition of 1851 was staged in London's Hyde Park and symbolised Britain's economic supremacy with the aid of an enormous glass and iron building casually dubbed 'the Crystal Palace', a name which stuck.

Its designer was a well-known garden architect, Joseph Paxton, who worked with engineer contractors Fox & Henderson to build the mother of all greenhouses, an iron and wood frame filled with panes of glass. It is still difficult to envisage the scale of the task they undertook: a mighty behemoth composed of vast numbers of small elements. No lesser commentator than Charles Dickens recounted the minutiae of the task for a contemporary magazine:

'Two parties in London, relying on the accuracy and good faith of certain iron-masters, glass-workers in the provinces, and of one master carpenter in London, bound themselves for a certain sum, to cover 18 acres of ground, with a building upwards of a third of a mile long (1851 feet, the exact date of the year) and some 450 broad. In order to do this, the glass-maker promised to supply in the required time nine hundred thousand square feet of glass (weighing more than four hundred tons) in separate panes, and these the largest that were ever made in sheet glass, each being 49 inches long. The iron-master gave his word in a like manner, to cast in due time 3,300 iron columns, varying from 14 ft. to 20 ft. in length; 34 miles of guttering tube, to join every individual column together, under the ground; 2,224 girders; besides 1,128 bearers for supporting galleries. The carpenter undertook to get ready within the specified period 205 miles of sash bar, flooring for an area of 33 millions of cubic feet; besides enormous quantities of wooden paling, louvre work and partition'.

Even, it seems, the great social moralist of the age could become entranced by such dizzying expenditure, such profligate invention, such scale of pride.

The objects on display came from all parts of the world, reflecting the scale of the British Empire including India and countries with recent white settlements like Australia and New Zealand. The number of exhibitors was about 14,000, nearly half of whom were non-British. France sent 1,760 exhibits and America 560. Among the American exhibits were a Colt repeating pistol, false teeth, Goodyear india-rubber products, chewing tobacco, and McCormick's reaping machine. Over six million visitors went to the exhibition, which eventually showed a total profit of $750,000.

right From Dickinson's *Comprehensive Pictures of the Great Exhibition*, Queen Victoria opening the Exhibition, here in the Foreign Nave of the Crystal Palace

Industrial Change: A Chronology

1709: Abraham Darby introduced coke smelting.

1712: The first workable steam-powered engine was developed.

1730: The seed drill was invented, freeing labour from the fields and lowering crop prices.

1740: Steel manufacturing using a crucible was discovered.

1759: The Canal Act was passed by the British Parliament leading to a national network of inland waterways for transport and industrial supplies.

1763: The spinning jenny, which effectively automated cotton spinning, was invented.

1765: James Watt perfected the steam engine.

1785: The power loom marked the start of the mechanised textile industry.

1785–99: Techniques of mass production of interchangeable parts were developed by the arms industry in the USA.

1797: The first industrial lathe was invented more or less simultaneously in England and the USA.

1802: The first electric battery capable of mass production was designed by William Cruickshank in England.

1811–16: A movement of workers in

Nottinghamshire, England, known as Luddites staged widespread protests against low pay and unemployment brought on by the introduction of mechanisation, involved destroying new machines.

1812: The population of Manchester, England passed 100,000.

1813: For the first time industrial employment overtook agricultural employment in England.

1825: The first regular railway services started between Stockton and Darlington in NE England.

1829: English engineer George Stephenson won a contest to design locomotives for the new Manchester-Liverpool railway.

1831–52: British industrial production doubled.

1832: The Reform Act concerning elections to the British Parliament gave representation to the industrial cities.

1833: The first effective Factory Act was passed in Britain regulating child labour in cotton mills.

c. 1840: The USA became the world leader for railroads, with over 3,000 miles laid.

1842: Cotton-industry workers in England staged a widespread strike.

1846: Repeal of the Corn Law in Britain reduced agricultural prices, further helping industry.

The Crystal Palace

In 1849 Prince Albert, husband of Queen Victoria and president of the Royal Society of Arts, decided to invite exhibitors from what were deemed the 'civilised nations' to participate in an exhibition. Funds were raised rapidly with Queen Victoria as a major subscriber, Paxton was appointed and the giddy adventure of The Crystal Palace was embarked upon.

The building itself took on the appearance of a very contemporary cathedral, with its long rectangular form intersected in the middle by a vaulted transept. Composed of an intricate network of slender iron rods sustaining walls of clear glass, the main body of the building was 562 metres long and 137 metres wide rising to a height of 32 metres in the central transept.

In fact it was like nothing on earth, except of course the horticultural greenhouses upon which it was based, but even these it left behind because of its scale which suggested, among other things, that it was potentially infinite. Its pre-fabricated elements meant that it could easily have been extended – as it later was – or transported to another site – as it also was – by the same facility that had enabled it to be built in the first place: railway transport.

The building was a remarkable success on every level. Vast and yet composed of elements small enough for human beings to relate to, it thrilled everyone who entered it with its sheer unreality: distances were impossible to calculate inside the endless repetitive crystal tunnels. Unadorned it would have impressed, but the Superintendent of the Works, an architect named Owen Jones, was charged with the task of enhancing the architectural effect of the limitless glass by adding colour.

This he did with an extravagant internal colour scheme of red, yellow and blue stripes separated by white bands, a touch which might have been over-egging the pudding but which seemed to impress both visitors and critics even more, one of them observing in a newspaper article that the interior of The Crystal Palace seemed like '*A Midsummer Night's Dream* seen in the clear light of midday'.

The Crystal Palace set the standard for later international fairs and exhibitions, most of which were also held in glass conservatories. Coming in quick succession were the New York City expositions of 1853, the Munich Exhibition of 1854, and the Paris Exposition of 1855.

The Crystal Palace's own subsequent history was fittingly weird. Taken down and re-erected with new extensions at Sydenham in South London, it was a venue for shows, exhibitions, concerts, football matches and other entertainments until, on the night of Nov. 30, 1936, it was virtually destroyed by fire. Twin towers that survived at either end of the building stood until 1941 when they were demolished in case they offered guidance to German bombers.

The Great Exhibition occurred in the middle of a century that saw many changes in the fabric of the city. And none of these changes was greater than the advent of the railways which, quite apart from changing the possibilities of travel to a dramatic degree, also put new markers in the city that changed its character and geometry. Their profound effects are still being felt today.

far left Inside the Crystal Palace after it had relocated to Sydenham, South London, in 1852

above While it was still in Hyde Park, visitors walking past the flowerbeds of the Crystal Palace during the 1851 Exhibition

The Railway: a Chronology

1804: Richard Trevithick built the first steam locomotive, using it on tracks at ironworks in South Wales.

1825: George Stephenson in England built the first public railway to carry steam trains – the Stockton and Darlington line – using his engine Locomotion .

1829: Stephenson designed a new locomotive called Rocket .

1830: Stephenson completed the Liverpool and Manchester Railway, the first steam passenger line. In the same year the first American-built locomotive, Best Friend of Charleston, went into service on the South Carolina Railroad.

1835: Germany pioneered steam railways in Europe, using Der Adler, yet another locomotive built by Stephenson.

1863: Robert Fairlie, a Scot, patented a locomotive with pivoting driving bogies, allowing tight curves in the track. In the same year London opened the world's first underground railway, powered initially by steam.

1869: The first US transcontinental railway was completed at Promontory, Utah, when the Union Pacific and the Central Pacific railroads met.

1879: The world's first public electric railway – Volk's Electric Railway – runs along the Brighton seafront in England.

1890: The first electric underground railway opened in London.

the railway station

Where the railway tracks met the inner city an enclosure and an introduction were required: an entrance, a place to arrange transit, a waiting space, a place to arrive and a place to depart – and something to celebrate an invention that seemed like a miracle to many The railway station quickly became a compendium of building possibilities: by definition it was something which would surely use the new iron technology that had made the railways possible in the first place; it was also a utilitarian place that could afford to be as eclectic as it liked; and it was a processing shed, somewhere to marshal not only the trains themselves but unprecedented numbers of often inexperienced railway travellers. There was no historical model and, from the outset, there were two apparently incompatible requirements inherent in the brief: the need to house trains and the need to accommodate human beings.

The trains themselves demanded vast interior spaces in every direction – up, so that the steam and smoke might disperse before choking everyone, and across, so that several trains and platforms could be accommodated side by side. The solution here was usually to adapt the iron and glass roof, sometimes partially open or louvred, so that large scale protection from the elements could be afforded to the trains and the passengers when getting on and off.

Otherwise the passengers needed facilities of a quite different scale and type. Smaller internal spaces were needed, scaled and arranged to accommodate human beings not mighty machines. In terms of the exterior, if the station building was to resemble anything from cities of the past it would be the city gate – but a city gate that often penetrated right to the heart of the city, exactly where a city gate was never traditionally sited.

Architects set about finding appropriate means of expression for the passenger stations and terminals whilst engineers tackled the structurally more daunting challenge of creating the necessary huge free spans that were now needed. And here at least there was some sort of precedent, that of the bridge.

A number of structural options existed: trusswork, cantilevers and the trusswork arch. However different locations required different solutions. A station, despite popular misuse of the word, is a stop on a route which continues beyond it; the big city centre stations are often properly described as terminals – the end of the line, or the beginning of it. It was terminals, then, that usually posed the biggest challenges having, as they did, to accommodate many trains side by side.

It was therefore the terminals that needed to span the biggest areas, and this they usually did with repetitive series of trusswork arches joined with longitudinal ribs and covering the resulting structure with glass in iron frames to make a glazed iron vault.

New Street Station, built in Birmingham, England in 1854 (and a genuine station, in this instance), achieved an iron truss roof with a span of 64 metres – one of the greatest spans ever recorded. It was to be eclipsed though by St. Pancras Station built in London in 1873, which featured a glazed hall spanned by 74-metre trussed iron arches. It was the largest undivided space ever enclosed and made more dramatic by the fact that the vault began at platform level, shooting up from exactly where passengers stood and arcing over nine or ten tracks to meet the platform on the other side in a similar arrangement. Although the St Pancras span was only ever exceeded by a few feet, it later became common practice to produce multiple sheds, side by side. Leipzig station, built 30 years later, managed a total width of 300 metres by this method.

Meanwhile the feature of the railway that was to have such lasting impact upon towns and cities – the passenger building – was developing in a spirit of unfettered architectural daydreaming. If the sheds were constrained by practicalities, the rest of the station building was constrained by nothing but it was fired by the spirit of 19th century eclecticism. Thus came stations that seemed to have been transported direct from Egypt, Italy, Greece or regions unknown to geography.

Today its loss is much lamented, but the Euston Arch – a mighty propylaeum worthy of Athens – that stood at the entrance to Euston Station must have raised the most undemanding traveller's expectations to a level that was unlikely to be satisfied by actual journey. Three and a half thousand miles away the modest Connecticut town of New Haven once boasted a station front resembling a mixture of Xanadu and Coney Island.

There were various solutions to the perceived problem of what to do with the shed. The Gare de l'Est in Paris plays with the forms of cathedral and palace before showing its hand with an open front that could only be a station, and a half rose window that could only be the end elevation of a train shed. Two stations separated by the width of a single road in London took markedly different approaches: St Pancras completely hides its world-beating span behind a High Gothic hotel, while neighbouring King's Cross incorporates its twin shed arches very conspicuously into its façade.

The impact of the railway station on towns and cities of all sizes would be lasting, whether as new symbols of escape from small towns, or new neighbourhood focal points for cities, encouraging a whole range of 'support structure' building – hotels, pubs, transport links, and even a certain transitory ambience in local residential, retail and business areas.

far left A steam train in the 1940s pulling into London's St.Pancras Station, which had remained virtually unaltered since the 19th century

left The stunning cathedral-like forms of the Gare de l'Est railway station concourse in Paris

To many in the 19th century though, railway stations and even demountable exhibition buildings, were vulgar distractions from the high purpose of 'real' architecture.

a multiplicity of styles

Since the beginning of the century several powerful strands of architectural thought had not been derailed by the coming of the industrial age, just modified by it or, in some cases, polarised to pursue even more traditionally-influenced styles.

The Gothic Revival remained popular In Britain from 1840 and 1870 when the appeal of its ecclesiastical overtones eventually gave way to the homelier charm of the Queen Anne Revival.

From early in the century towns had been expanded with numerous buildings in the international Greek Revival manner such as William Wilkins' Yorkshire Museum, York (1827–30).

Alfred Waterhouse, having experimented with Gothic Revival in Manchester Town Hall produced the much-admired Romanesque-inspired Natural History Museum, (1873–81, London).

The architect Charles Robert Cockerell mixed elements from Greek, Roman, Renaissance and Baroque architecture in a surprisingly successful synthesis for his master work the Ashmolean Museum and Taylorian Institution, Oxford (1841–45). He also produced some distinctive commercial buildings, notably the Bank of England, Liverpool (1844–47).

In Europe the new technologies were being incorporated in similar although sometimes intriguingly different ways. Labrouste's Bibliothèque Ste.-Geneviève had come about as a result of the theories expressed by the French writer/architect Viollet-le-Duc in his *Entretiens sur l'architecture*, namely that the basic principles of Gothic architecture were not inimical to new technological processes. France took to iron and steel

below left Victorian grandeur in provincial England: the Town Hall, Manchester, designed by Alfred Waterhouse in 1877

below right The Natural History Museum, Cromwell Road, London, also designed by Waterhouse

enthusiastically, none more so than Gustave Eiffel (1832–1932) who before giving the world one of its most famous landmarks had built a stunning viaduct at Garabit, France, as well as the frame of the Statue of Liberty.

The Eiffel Tower belonged to the same thinking as the Great Exhibition in Hyde Park; it was outrageous – and it certainly outraged many at the time – but it was also good enough to outlast fashionable opprobrium or acclaim. Four huge, tapering, lattice-girder piers rise from a huge base square and are laced together at two levels by connecting girders. Immensely rigid, the Tower was assumed to be unsafe by many Parisians most of whom hated its impact on their city. To allay their unfounded fears, some structurally useless but visually stabilising ironwork decoration was added (and later removed) along with the non-functional arches at the base which remain. One famous literary figure hated it so much that he said he always dined at its restaurant since that was the only place in Paris from which he could not see the monstrosity.

In Amsterdam The Rijksmuseum took on a Renaissance form behind which lurked large internal courts of iron and glass. Meanwhile in Austria and Germany the same preoccupations with structure and style were being played out. Classical styles dominated in the period before the dissolution of the Austro-Hungarian Empire typified by Gothic churches such as Heinrich von Ferstel's Votivkirche in Vienna (1856–79). In Germany, buoyed on a wave of rising national confidence, activity ranged from the definitive museum plan, Munich's Alte Pinakothek (Old Pinakothek) by Leo von Klenze, to a series of Disney-esque palaces built for the deranged Ludwig II of Bavaria who loathed the industrial age and set about ruining himself with the spiralling cost of the palaces of Linderhof, Herrenchiemsee and Neuschwanstein.

École des Beaux-Arts

The École des Beaux-Arts (School of Fine Arts) in Paris was the most important centre of architectural education in the Western world in the 19th century. A complex organisation, it was housed in a group of buildings on the Left Bank of the Seine and represented a strong aesthetic tradition within which existed the most powerful cultural force that had ever been set in place to train architects.

Founded in 1819 as the successor to the Royal Academy of Architecture, the École drew students not only from France but also from throughout Europe and – after 1850 – from North America.

The school treated architecture as a public service, a medium for realising in three dimensions the abstracts of national and civic pride.

Its methods were to establish architectural ideals through study of the five orders in Rome, and – a strictly local touch – the expression of such ideals in 17th century France.

Jacques-Ignace Hittorff was typical of those architects who combined the practice of modern classicism with archaeological investigation into Roman and Greek architecture. His Gare du Nord, Paris (1861–65), showed brilliantly how a classical architectural language could be adapted to celebrate a major metropolitan railway terminal. At Saint-Vincent-de-Paul, Paris, Hittorff incorporated the multi-coloured decoration inspired by his

Eugène-Emmanuel Viollet-le-Duc
1814–1879

Eugène-Emmanuel Viollet-le-Duc was a remarkably influential French Gothic Revival architect and restorer of French medieval buildings. However it was not his buildings but his copiously expressed theories of rational architectural design linking traditional styles to new functional materials that ensured his influence.

Viollet-le-Duc certainly dominated 19th-century theories of architectural restorationn claiming always to restore in the style of the original despite a regrettable later tendency to add new elements of his own.

Viollet-le-Duc's broad architectural thesis was published in his book *Entretiens sur l'architecture* which contained information on the construction of iron frames enclosed by masonry curtain walls, and greatly influenced the late 19th-century architects of the Chicago School. Other influential writings by Viollet-le-Duc included *L'Art russe* and *De la décoration appliquée aux édifices* ('On Decoration Applied to Buildings').

famous discovery that Greek temples had been not bone white as originally supposed, but actually painted in strong colours.

Henri Labrouste, a highly thoughtful architect, used the Beaux-Arts perspective to translate Greek architecture into accessible, human spaces. It was not a well-received theory until he gave it form in a great public building : the Library of Ste.-Geneviève, Paris.

The architectural system of the Beaux-Arts was uniquely hard to acquire. Although it used some traditional examination methods, any attempts to duplicate its curriculum and testing methods were doomed to fail. This was because the Beaux-Arts intentionally invented itself as a unique pyramidal organisation: at the base was the general level of access that anyone with talent might use; at the top, the zenith of a complex internal obstacle race, was a single prize: the Prix de Rome, involving study in Rome and a more or less guaranteed career of building major public

monuments. By this time he would have completed a course lasting 15 years and would have built nothing whatsoever. Only after completing five years in Rome would the lucky winner be allowed to build something that was guaranteed by the single-mindedness of his education, to be nothing other than a Beaux-Arts Neoclassical building.

The Paris Opéra

Charles Garnier's Paris Opera House (1862–75) is widely regarded as the high point of 19th-century French Classicism. It was and remains a quite overpowering building, often compared in the scale of its urban impact with the Colosseum of Ancient Rome. Like the Colosseum it was intended as more than just a simple venue for entertainment. It was intended by Garnier as an elaborate setting in which both performers and audience appeared in a high celebration of cultural awareness. One has only to think

above From a series of eleven photographs following the progress of the building of the Eiffel Tower in Paris, taken through 1888 and 1889

above Masks of tragedy and comedy surround a statue of Apollo with his lyre, the crowning glory of the Paris Opera House

below The grand staircase at the Paris Opera, splendid affluence epitomised in luxurious design

back to Bernini's Saint Theresa tableau in the church of Santa Maria della Vittoria to recall a small scale version of the same phenomenon. There it was the worshipper being drawn in to a sculptural theatre; at the Paris Opera House the psychology was the same, but the canvas was larger and now the Church was nowhere to be seen. The new agenda was set by the bourgeoisie and its values were their values. This was no accident, since the Opera House was conceived very much as part of Haussmann's new Paris. The old layout of the city made Notre Dame Cathedral its focal point; Haussmann's Paris might have been designed for the specific purpose of drawing the maximum number of citizens to La Place de l' Opèra.

Self-consciously cathedral-like in its scale and form, Garnier's building features many highly eclectic effects, touches of Michelangelo, a reprise of the east façade of the Louvre and numerous celebratory sculptures of the great and the good, as in medieval cathedrals, but here using secular heroes – actual composers as well as allegorical figures drawn from the realm of musical mythology.

The final grand gesture of the Opera House is its extraordinary size. It is 182 metres long, 91 metres wide and rises in places to a height of 60 metres. Since the auditorium, restricted by the demands of sightlines and acoustics, is not unusually large, one wonders initially why such a vast exterior was needed for such a small interior. The truth is that Garnier chose, like Haussmann, to seize an opportunity to reinvent with both hands, adding to his grand architectural gesture many practical internal features: a huge stage out of all proportion to the auditorium, dressing rooms, a large rehearsal facility and numerous administrative areas.

The planning and spatial complexity of the Opèra owe much to Beaux-Arts methods of organisation, but the scale is new, as is the lavish provision of circulation space, including the great staircase and numerous richly decorated galleries, foyers, and corridors.

In his writings Garnier made much of the practicalities of his building and of his own pragmatic approach. He noted, for example, that at the opera people tend to walk in pairs, and this observation had determined the width of circulation areas. He also noted that since women tended to arrive by coach, the appropriate entrance was given a more 'feminine' style of decoration and furnished with numerous mirrors.

Like so many of the 19th century advocates of classicism, Garnier was also proud of what technology could add to his vision, notably the Opèra's mechanical ventilation system and its elevators.

However, the defining images of this extraordinary building are those of its triumphant exterior and densely-appointed internal arrival spaces, all huge columns, candelabra, statuary, gilt and relentless gloire.

haussmann's reinvented paris

It is rare that a major city gets a complete overhaul. When it does it gives valuable insights into contemporary attitudes towards the city form; that is what happened in the mid-19th century to what is today regarded as one of the world's finest cities. Well into the century that had already seen amazing improvements in technology and engineering feats, some areas

of Paris had not been improved in any significant way for hundreds of years. It was not an uncommon story. As we have seen, despite an unalloyed appetite for grand gestures, noble country homes, fine palaces and awe-inspiring churches, the rich and powerful rarely rediscovered Rome's obsessional zeal for making citizens feel like the owners of their city. As a result problems abounded in the Paris of the 1850s. Access from the centre of one locality to another was difficult. Even getting to the city's brand new gateways, its railway stations, was problematic for most people. The rapid pace of industrialisation – by no means unique to Paris – had resulted in overpopulation, squalor and misery. Since it was just such conditions that had contributed to the French Revolution, Napoleon III, who was Emperor from 1852 to 1870 in the period following the Revolution, decided to take action. He had been further impelled to do so by the new dominant economic and political force, the middle and upper middle classes. They were demanding rather more than an upgrade of basic utilities. In addition to hospitals, schools and parkland, they wanted

right An aerial view of Paris centred on the Arc de Triomphe, and showing clearly how Haussmann's grand plan for the city was realised

libraries and theatres too; in fact they wanted a genuinely civilised urban environment in which to work and enjoy their leisure. The agent of change was to be Napoleon's prefect of the Seine, Baron Georges-Eugène Haussmann, a lawyer and administrator without whom Napoleon's grandest ambitions could never have been realised.

Haussmann was the creator of what we see today when we look at Paris. Given planning power on a grand scale he responded accordingly, proposing straight, arterial thoroughfares, symmetrical compositions, and elaborately contrived vistas. With an almost surgical approach he cut directly through the rat's nest of the slums with large boulevards, established modern sewer and water systems fed by a system of aqueducts, stripped the Île de la Cité to the bone, replaced the old market district with a new iron complex Les Halles Centrale, installed gas lighting, built four new bridges across the Seine and replaced three old ones. In addition he created a network of small parks throughout the city where space was at a premium and reserved five larger areas of parkland for districts around the periphery. There were new hospitals and asylums, created on a scale that seems almost unimaginable today; also new schools, administrative centres and prisons sprang up as well. The grand Louvre Palace was expanded, the École des Beaux-Arts was enlarged, the national library was completed and, most significantly, a great new opera house was conceived.

Haussmann's planning system was as thoughtful as it was bold. Practical and eclectic, Haussmann contrived three modes of street planning borrowed from various historical models but, taken together, resembling none of them. Firstly there was a crossing of main axial streets. Secondly there were two concentric rings originally defined by the old city walls and now promoted into ring roads. Finally there were avenues defined by nothing except the pragmatic need to link established points of activity in the city – for example market places and transport depots.

Politics never being far away from any town planning decision, Haussmann's plan also took care to ensure that new wide boulevards sliced through those areas of eastern Paris that had so recently fomented revolution. The new system meant that not only would any future fighting behind the barricades in narrow streets be curtailed, troop movements would be facilitated by new routes leading directly from barracks to potential trouble spots. In the wealthy west of the city Haussmann's broad boulevards were adapted to a building programme of residential properties and also encouraged the spread of shops, outdoor social areas and promenading.

All cities are constantly being reinvented, but it is rare indeed that a major city renovation of such scale is tried in circumstances other than that of total destruction. That Haussmann's Paris should have been executed with such vision, practical concern and self-confidence is as much as a monument to the human urge to urbanise as the city itself, which can be said to have stood the test of time triumphantly. That it happened in a century that was already laying the foundations for a very different new technological world was as much a coincidence of spirit as a response in purely material terms.

Georges-Eugène Haussmann
1809–1891

Born in 1809 in Paris, France, Haussmann will always be remembered as the administrator responsible for the redesign of Paris in the mid-19th century. Through this he indirectly exerted enormous influence on the design of cities all over the world.

Haussmann studied law in Paris and entered the civil service in 1831 as the secretary-general of a prefecture, rising to be subprefect, prefect in the provinces and finally prefect of the Seine département, which post he was holding when handed his great commission.

Haussmann's extraordinary success in implementing a new plan for Paris was made possible by the autocratic nature of Napoleon's regime, since this allowed him to take out large long-term loans and use them almost without any parliamentary or other control. His handling of public money, however, attracted increasing criticism among the political opponents, and when a liberal government finally came to power in 1870 Haussmann was quickly dismissed.

Perhaps in response Haussmann became a Bonapartist member for Corsica in the National Assembly from 1877 to 1881, although there is little evidence that he had any great appetite for politics without power; his major, permanent, achievement already lay behind him, a unique blend of architectural vision and political pragmatism.

towards a new
architecture

Sagrada Familia Temple, Barcelona

10

upward mobility

In retrospect it seems almost as if the Neoclassical adventures of the mid- to late-19th century were a calculated postponement of the inevitable. There was little organised thought concerning the use of the new technologies to create identifiably modern cities. Numerous individual experiments were almost always the result of efforts by gifted or visionary individuals. There had been no collective decision to convert the grand adventures of The Crystal Palace or the Eiffel Tower into a rational built environment, or even to use their examples as a starting point for a new way of looking at buildings.

However, from about 1880 onwards architectural thought began to coalesce on both sides of the Atlantic into the beginnings of a series of experiments that would change the shapes of towns and cities forever.

Suddenly growth was everywhere. Fuelled by new prosperity, towns and cities began to grow in size at a breakneck speed. Europe was still unsettled and, as it turned out, rightly apprehensive about political instability, and so the sense of excitement about the approach of a new century was tempered with nervousness. In America though there was no such concern. Instead there was the boundless vigour of a new country founded on pioneer stock that suddenly finds itself with a whole new technology to build with. Anything was possible, and the only unknown was how quickly it might be achieved.

Eventually an architectural revolution got underway in America; its focal point was the 'windy city' of Chicago, Illinois, and as always there was a link with the immediate past.

Henry Hobson Richardson, born in 1838 and raised in the American south, was the initiator of Romanesque revival in the United States and a pioneer figure in the development of an indigenous modern American style of architecture. Whilst studying at Harvard he decided to become an architect. There were no schools of architecture in America before the Civil War, but, being fluent in French from his Louisiana upbringing, he studied at the École des Beaux-Arts in Paris until the Civil War at home meant his income was cut off, at which point he went to work in the architectural office of Théodore Labrouste.

After the Civil War ended he returned to America and began his own practice, winning a competition in 1866 to design the Church of the Unity in Springfield, Massachusetts.

His practice duly launched, Richardson moved to New York City for some years, forming a partnership that took over some of the administrative load allowing him to design a series of public buildings and churches in upstate New York and Boston.

Richardson's Romanesque revival designs won him national fame, and enough New England commissions to encourage him to move to the Boston area where, in suburban Brookline, he bought an early 19th-century house redolent of the plantation houses of the Deep South. There he worked to create many of the buildings upon which his reputation was built. His best and most famous commercial structure was the Marshall Field Wholesale Store in Chicago, which was to become the inspiration and model for a generation of Chicago architects.

below H.H. Richardson's typical Romanesque design in the Austin Hall at his old Alma Mater, Harvard

Little of Richardson's built work survives, a notable exception being The Crane Library in Quincy, Massachusetts, built between 1880 and 1883. Featuring a tripartite layering of a rough-faced granite base beneath continuous clerestory windows topped with a tiled gable roof, the Crane Library is an informal but cleverly arranged mass of detail recombined from its classical past into a very personal style. The cavern-like entrance arch creates a sense of occasion that remains in keeping with the scale of the whole building.

By the time Richardson died in 1886 he had earned a national reputation and exerted influence on many through a personal style that was very heavy but nonetheless always well-managed and proportioned.

Of his admirers it was to be the Chicago School that responded first with buildings that reflected their admiration. Their opportunity came as the result of a serious fire that swept through Chicago in 1871, destroying several cast iron buildings and demonstrating the need for steel to replace cast iron in any new structures. The widespread damage demanded a major rebuilding programme at just that point in building technology development, when the skyscraper was emerging as a viable building type. It had been possible to build high for some time, but the results would have been extremely impractical for use until the timely invention of the electric-powered elevator.

Leading contender for title of the first skyscraper was the ten-storey Home Insurance Building in Chicago, built between 1883 and 1885. Arguably it had been pre-dated by James Bogardus' five-storey Cast Iron Building (1848, New York City) in which the weight of construction was borne by columns, rather than the walls. Generally though the Bogardus building technique was regarded as an important step towards the genuine skyscraper, which the Home Insurance Building certainly was, having a steel-girder construction faced with a curtain wall. (A curtain wall is defined as an outer covering of masonry or other material that carries only its own weight since the steel skeleton carrying the building loads simply has the curtain wall material fixed to it).

Architect of the Home Insurance Building was William le Baron Jenney, and although he was unable to escape from traditional exterior detailing or indeed a traditional building shape, he had taken the first important step in founding what would become known as the Chicago School.

above The imposing façade of a church by H.H.Richardson in Boston, Massachusetts

skyscrapers

The term 'skyscraper' originally applied to buildings of 10 to 20 stories, but by the late 20th century the term was used to describe high-rise buildings of exceptional height, generally greater than 40 or 50 storeys.

Skyscrapers became necessary because of the increase in urban commerce in the United States in the second half of the 19th century. Cities could no longer expand horizontally at will, although the obvious solution of expanding vertically did not become a reality until the installation of the first safe passenger in 1857 in a New York department store. The earliest tall buildings rested on extremely thick masonry walls

at the ground level, but architects soon realised that if a cast-iron and wrought-iron framework could support the weight of the upper floors it would leave more floor space free on lower levels.

The refinement of a technique for mass-producing steel – the Bessemer process – suddenly opened up new possibilities allowing for a major advance in skyscraper construction. Steel is stronger and lighter than iron, and it was a steel frame that supported William Le Baron Jenney's 10-storey Home Insurance Company Building in Chicago.

As the population density of urban areas has increased, so has the need for buildings that rise rather than spread. The skyscraper, originally exclusively a form of commercial architecture, has increasingly been adapted for residential buildings too.

the chicago school

None of the so-called Chicago School architects actually came from that city. Rootless Americans who gravitated to where the work was, they were very much of their time. The movement's six major names soon fell into three teams: John Wellborn Root joined Daniel Burnham; William Holabird joined Martin Roche; and Dankmar Adler joined Louis Sullivan.

Between them, these three teams of complementary talents laid down the basics of not only the Chicago school but also of 20th century commercial architecture. Inspired by the architectural rationalism of Viollet-le-Duc, they each sought a better aesthetic expression of the metal frame building.

Among their more successful attempts was the Reliance Building by Daniel Burnham who in 1895 just after his partner's death, charged another member of the firm, Charles B. Atwood, with the design. The framework of the top ten storeys was accomplished in little over two weeks and the result was a building that took a giant step forward into visually light skyscrapers. Earlier the same firm had produced the notable Monadnock Building in Chicago, another behemoth but masonry-built with the drawback of tiny windows punched through too solid walls.

Holabird & Roche produced Chicago's Marquette Building in 1893, less airy than the Reliance Building but carrying its monumentality very well in a quasi-classical way.

Perhaps the least evenly-matched of the three leading Chicago School partnerships was that of Louis Sullivan and Dankmar Adler, the former being something of a poetic visionary, the latter a tough-minded engineer. Sullivan was the more powerful spirit, another architect with so much on his mind that buildings were not enough – copious writings followed, from which we get Sullivan's famous dictum 'form follows function'.

Heavily influenced by Richardson's Marshall Field Store, Sullivan sought to reprise it in his Auditorium Building of 1887–9, in which a multi-purpose structure (it was to be hotel, theatre and office building all in one) rose ten storeys to resemble a stripped down version of Marshall Field, robbed of its heavy decorative effects but confirmed in its coherent and well-articulated form.

One of Sullivan's most celebrated skyscrapers was the Guaranty Building in Buffalo, New York. He built it in 1895 and developed the theory for it in an essay published in Lippincott's Magazine. His stated aim was to create a visually light, 13-storey skyscraper that combined rich detailing with the illusion of soaring height. Back in Chicago he took this ambition one step further with the Schlesinger & Meyer Department store, later to be re-christened the Carson, Pirie, Scott Department Store. Here was another prototype in the making – the harbinger of innumerable department stores and office buildings to follow.

The Schlesinger & Meyer store comprised 10 floors of offices covered with white terracotta tiles hung, curtain wall style, onto the massive frame. This expanse in punctuated with regular rows of large windows. These offices are built on top of two storeys given over to the shop which is itself framed by part of the metal structure – an open declaration of construction method mixed with rich decorative effects. The towered corner of the store marked the high point of the whole affair as the entrance was made highly invitational by means of rich, naturalistic ornament. Sullivans's plan was clear: the nature of the building should not be disguised, but equally it should not resist any distinctive decorative effects that helped enhance its structural means.

To the inhabitants of Chicago and, soon, to a growing number of American cities, there was a growing awareness that 'architecture' and perhaps more importantly 'architectural theory' was no longer confined to great churches or even to great railway stations, but that moves were afoot to make it part of everyday life.

New York City

New York, built on solid rock, rapidly became the natural home of skyscrapers, despite Chicago's early lead. Even so the two cities' architects interchanged rather less frequently than might be imagined. Louis Sullivan, for example, was responsible for just one building in New York, the charming Bayard Building on Bleecker Street.

Not too far away from the Bayard is a more spectacular example of the Chicago School in New York: The Flatiron Building.

Elevators

The widespread acceptance of the elevator, or lift, played a key role in creating the characteristic urban geography of many modern cities by making high-rise buildings a practical possibility for the first time.

Lifting building materials by mechanical means goes back at least as far as Roman times. In the first century B.C. Vitruvius described lifting platforms powered by human beings, animals, or water and using pulleys and capstans.

Steam power was applied to lifting devices in England by 1800 and by the early 19th century a hydraulic type of lift was introduced, in which the platform was attached to a plunger in a cylinder sunk in the ground beneath the shaft to a depth equal to the shaft's height. Fluid in the subterranean cylinder was pressurized by a steam pump.

Such devices employed counterbalances so reducing the amount of force that was needed to raise the load.

Until the middle of the 19th century these principles were confined to freight lifting – the unreliability of the hemp ropes used for hoisting made them inadvisable for passenger use.

When Elisha Graves Otis introduced a safety device in 1853, he made the passenger elevator possible. Otis' device involved a clamping feature that would grab the car's guide rails if tension was lost from the hoist rope.

The first passenger elevator – steam driven – was installed in the Haughwout Department Store in New York City in 1857 where it climbed five storeys in under a minute with no fatalities.

Elevator technology improved but remained locked into steam propulsion for 30 years until the introduction of the electric motor for elevator operation in 1880, manufactured by Siemens. This used the motor to drive a cable-winding drum in the building's basement.

The first commercial installation was in the Demarest Building in New York City in 1889.

The introduction of electricity quickly led to a near perfection of elevator technology: in 1894 push-button controls were introduced, and a year later in England a hoisting apparatus was tested that applied the power to the pulley at the top of the shaft – the weights of the car and the counterweights were sufficient to ensure traction. This removed limitations imposed by the winding drum method, making possible taller shafts and faster journeys.

left Louis Sullivan's Carson, Pirie, Scott department store in Chicago

below The façade of Sullivan's famed Guaranty Building in Buffalo

The Flatiron Building

In 1904 at an acute intersection of Fifth Avenue and Broadway was erected the Fuller Building, and it was to become at once the city's most famous skyscraper. It was built by D. H. Burnham & Co, a company formed after the death of Daniel Burnham's partner John Welborn Root, and it is a building that affects everyone who sees it for one simple reason: its dramatic wedge shape makes it a natural piece of architectural theatre. It is natural because its plan conforms precisely to that of the awkward wedge-shaped site, in itself a rare thing in grid-like New York where, north of Greenwich Village, only the meandering diagonal of Broadway causes such irregularities. However, Burnham's solution can hardly be called obvious. Its shape creates dynamic effects: whichever angle you view it from, the building (which immediately lost its official name in favour of the informally descriptive one of 'the Flatiron') looks to be of a different volume. From one angle it appears as little more than a thick wall hiding nothing; from another it looks as solid as its more conventional block-deep neighbours.

The Flatiron Building, though, has other claims to being a distinguished member of the iron-frame curtain-walled newcomers to Manhattan at the turn of the century. It is a decidedly lively building, with more than a touch of French Renaissance detailing, and what could have been a boring mass is broken up by some very well-considered effects. Its highly-detailed limestone façade features some gently curved bays in the mid section to avoid the sheer-wall effect that might otherwise have made the building oppressive from certain angles.

New York would soon become awash with skyscrapers, many of them wildly imaginative confections of decorative flourishes pasted onto humdrum steel-frame towers. However, the city would have to wait almost 30 years, for The General Electric Building by Cross & Cross, before it saw another such imaginative example of fitting a skyscraper into an unpromising urban site. The General Electric Building sits adjacent to a Byzantine-style church – whose materials it emulates – and hides its base bulk behind the church, concentrating its effects upon an supremely elegant 51-storey decorated tower.

left Spectacular at any angle: the Flatiron Building at the intersection of Broadway and 5th Avenue, NYC

right Auguste Perret's concrete apartments, erected in the Rue Franklin, Paris, in 1903

Concrete

The discovery of ferro-concrete had been refined to a point where it could be confidently used in conjunction with the ever-more inventive experiments with steel frames. One of the earliest examples of its use was the church of St-Jean de Montmartre, Paris, France, (1897–1904) by Anatole de Baudot. Baudot was part of a tradition dedicated to introducing new technological developments to traditional structural techniques, Taking neo-Gothic as his starting point he created a church in which the form was reduced to its bare essentials by use of a new material. In doing so he set out the stall of future architects for whom the removal of unnecessary detail went hand in hand with a visual expression of the forms involved in creating a building.

The approach was taken further by Auguste Perret whose apartments of 1903 brought to 25 bis Rue Franklin, Paris, the next logical development of the steel frame building. The frame construction made it a simple matter to open up the building inside, introducing an unexpected but perfectly logical effect.

At the same time the frame was openly expressed on the outside despite being decorated with floral pattern tiles. A concrete block of apartments in 1903 set a fine precedent that, sadly, was to be subsequently poorly and cheaply reflected in so many concrete apartments buildings of the mid-century and beyond.

Two Stations

New York City has played host to two of the best station buildings ever conceived. Both were built just after the turn of the century, both embraced the new technology with great enthusiasm, both echoed the architecture of previous ages, and both brought an extraordinary degree of romance to railroad travel. One was demolished in an act of sanctioned vandalism in the 1960s that still outrages today; the other was saved – just – and continues as one of the city's grand public spaces even though its original importance as a terminal is much diminished.

Pennsylvania Station marked the peak of the output of the firm McKim, Mead & White. Constructed between 1902 and 1911 this, the original Pennsylvania Station (nothing like the mundane subterranean station that today sits beneath Madison Square Garden), sought to combine the classical splendour of ancient times with the practicality of modern railroad travel, and to do it embracing contemporary building methods on a site of nearly eight acres.

The result was a success that was simply never equalled. Its most remarked upon feature was the general waiting room, based on the tepidarium of the Baths of Caracalla but scaled up by 20 per cent. Steel-framed, travertine clad and with suspended plaster vaults it offered such a dazzling contrast to most transportation waiting rooms that the wonder is that anyone ever chose to leave it for the more prosaic surroundings of a train journey. The concourse reaffirmed the technology of the day with exclusively steel and glass construction although, like the general waiting room, this too was divided with three high vaults.

If Pennsylvania Station marked a high spot in city centre railway stations, Grand Central Terminal, just a few blocks away, came a close second. Much more compact and constrained by its site to offer no great sweeping frontage, Grand Central makes up for its modest exterior with a concourse that takes the breath away. Built by Reed & Stern and Warren & Wetmore, Grand Central – saved from the developers' wrecking ball only by intervention of the Supreme Court in the aftermath of Pennsylvania Station's loss – is the last word in station planning. It houses two levels of tracks designed to serve both commuter and main lines, a monumental Beaux-Arts concourse with a barrel vaulted ceiling featuring signs of the zodiac, and a famous meeting place by a central globe clock. No other station interior can quite match the impact of Grand Central's, with its ingeniously complex of ramps, arches and passageways linking levels and neighbouring streets in a calm, subdued cathedral-like atmosphere. This atmosphere is encouraged by low levels of lighting, both artificial and natural that filters through giant arched windows which reveal themselves to be monumentally double-glazed – wall-thick glass assemblies spaced widely enough apart to house connecting passageways.

left The spectacular effect of light streaming into the concourse of the Grand Central Station c.1930

right The interior court of Lloyd Wright's Larkin Building, Buffalo NY

far right An exterior view of the Larkin Building, 1905

Frank Lloyd Wright 1869–1959

In the year that Sullivan completed the Schlesinger & Meyer store, the junior member of the Chicago School erected a building in Buffalo, New York, that would take the new movement further than anything before. Frank Lloyd Wright's Larkin Building may have sounded like a humdrum project, being a bespoke office for a mail order firm, but it turned out to be a typically lucid building from one of architecture's true pioneer spirits. It was erected in 1904 next to the railway tracks. Sealed and fireproof, with filtered, conditioned, mechanical ventilation, it was equipped with metal desks, chairs, and files, furnished with sound-absorbent surfaces and given exceptionally well-balanced light, both natural and artificial. Externally it took on a block-like geometry, with secondary corner piers seeming to support a giant lintel formed by the top storey of galleries.

This highly unusual building was really a synthesis of the lessons of private houses (whose design had already occupied much of Wright's time and effort), and the skyscrapers on which he had also worked when employed by Louis Sullivan.

It prefigured not only the office blocks of a future age, but the kind of organizational thinking that would only much later filter down to corporations who would come to realise that the landscape of the workplace has profound implications for business efficiency.

Wright would go on to become the nonpareil great American architect with an oeuvre stretching over six decades and an influence that is still not fully analyzed.

He became known for 'organic architecture', in which buildings reflected their natural surroundings. For a decade before the Larkin Building he had been developing what would become his celebrated prairie house style, a series of low, spreading houses with projecting roofs. He later diversified, employing reinforced concrete to explore a variety of geometric forms.

Among his most famous buildings must count his Wisconsin home, Taliesin East, 1925, Falling Water, near Pittsburgh, Pennsylvania, 1936 – a house of cantilevered terraces straddling a waterfall – and the Guggenheim Museum, New York, 1959, with its a spiral ramp rising from a circular plan.

Back at the turn of the century Frank Lloyd Wright was already looking at spaces – both residential and commercial – with an architectural eye that could combine a highly sophisticated formal perception with a prodigious understanding of how buildings related to those who would actually have to use them.

art nouveau

Art Nouveau architects gave varied expression to many of the themes that had preoccupied the early 19th century. These ranged from Viollet-le-Duc's call plea structural honesty to Sullivan's demand for an organic architecture. In France unexpected forms appeared in iron, masonry, and concrete, notably the structures of Hector Guimard for the Paris Métro at the turn of the century, and the Samaritaine Department Store (1905) near the Pont Neuf in Paris, by Frantz Jourdain.

Art Nouveau came into being under a bewildering variety of national names: it was called Jugendstil in Germany, Stile Floreale (or Stile Liberty) in Italy, Modernismo (or Modernista) in Spain and Sezessionstil in Austria.

Dutch architect Hendrik Petrus Berlage worked in a fundamentalist almost moralistic manner, insisting on a return to honesty of materials. His major work, the Amsterdam Exchange (1897–1903) favours an external treatment executed in straightforward brick and stone, and an interior of brick, iron, and glass that becomes decorative in spite of its simplicity.

Finnish architect Eliel Saarinen (father of Eeero Saarinen who would design the wildly expressionistic TWA terminal at John F. Kennedy Airport) brought an Art Nouveau flavour to his Helsinki Railway Station (1906–14). There were also stylistic links between the work of the Art Nouveau designers in Vienna and in that of Charles Rennie Mackintosh in Glasgow, where his School of Art (1896–1909), remains one of the most dazzlingly original of all Art Nouveau buildings.

In Belgium the leading light of the new movement was Baron Victor Horta who had created, in his Brussels Hôtel Tassel of 1892, a complex series of levels, a sinuous façade all based on an octagonal geometry. And his later Hôtel Solvay embodies all the romantic characteristics of Art Nouveau in a bravura display of decorative wrought ironwork.

Horta's chief work, though, was the Maîson du Peuple in Brussels (1896–99), the first Belgium structure to have an iron and glass façade.

Hector Guimard, originator of the Paris Metro iron decorations, took his enthusiasm for Art Nouveau to fruition with the Castel-Béranger apartment building at 16 rue La Fontaine, Passy, Paris, where the façade was so richly decorated with writhing forms as to appear virtually alive.

Anything as heavily mannered as Art Nouveau, which enjoyed equal vogue in the fields of glass, jewellery and illustration, was doomed to be short-lived. Impractical for prosaic building needs, it declined rapidly in popularity and by 1910 was more or less exhausted. However, its claim to immortality was its recruitment Antonio Gaudí, a Barcelona-based architect whose enthusiasm for organic forms transcended the superficially decorative and promised to engulf entire buildings.

Gaudí's imaginative and theatrical experiments with space, form and ornament changed the face of his home city Barcelona which still reveres a highly organic collection of apartment buildings. These amazing structures include the Casa Milá apartment house (1905–10) and the residence of the Batlló family (1904–06).

Gaudí's grand personal project – unfinished at the moment he stepped in front of a moving tram in 1926 – was the truly bizarre Expiatory Temple of the Holy Family (Sagrada Familia) in Barcelona.

Wright Revisited

Frank Lloyd Wright's career was so long that it easily spanned the influential early years of the Chicago School and the middle years of the

20th century. If there is any link between the creative maelstrom of the early 1900s and the way The City would be shaped by the next upheavals in architectural thought, Wright provides it, by example, if not built achievement. He continued to build his extraordinary prairie houses and other residences too, always cutting through prevailing styles and bringing to bear his own remarkable skills at manipulating three-dimensional geometry. Manipulating three-dimensional geometry, after all, is what architecture is about, and in his domestic residences Wright virtually invented the concept of open plan, a form that would be re-interpreted endlessly in both commercial and domestic living spaces throughout the rest of the century.

In the early 1920s this Wisconsin-born architect built the Imperial Hotel in Tokyo which triumphantly survived an earthquake a few years later. He continued to explore spatial possibilities in projects that were always unpredictable but never embarked upon for superficial effect.

Wright was one of the few who would be able to continue such individualistic experiments as the past few decades had witnessed. A calamitous world war quickly changed the spirit of the times once again, this time preparing the ground for a more sober, less parochial view of the world and its built environment.

far left The Art Nouveau-inspired railway station at Helsinki, Finland

left The statues flanking the main entrance of Helsinki Railway Station

below left The incredilble detail of Gaudi's Sagrada Familia in Barcelona

below right The Sagrada Familia cathedral under construction

11

international moder

& the bauhaus

11

the city reborn

Anyone expecting the history of urban development to be a smooth and unbroken process will by now have realised that it is anything but that. If we look through the wrong end of the historical telescope we can see bursts of frenetic activity in which cities changed very rapidly, interrupted by often centuries-long periods of comparative inactivity while politicians and popes channeled their energies, ambitions, thought and money into a broadly retrospective and élite architecture, usually fashioned to match the historical moment and other short-term considerations but generally unmindful of the city fabric as a whole.

Of course, during these hiatuses the city still continued to develop the world over, according to local custom and need, as cities must. Incrementally improving, reconfiguring, lapsing, often disappearing through war or pestilence, and then starting all over again, cities never stand still even if there is no conscious ideological or technical force to drive or shape them. Such processes, though, are aimless and essentially anti-progressive; they are like moving the furniture round rather than remodelling the premises.

All the major changes in building design, and therefore in cities too, have come about as the result of a Big Idea. Human history is littered with Big Ideas both good and bad, and so it is with architecture. The verdicts of future generations inevitably change, and the style that is bad today is often seen as good tomorrow: for example, contrast the outrage that the Forth Bridge in Scotland provoked in the 1880s with the almost universal admiration it attracts today.

Therefore, as we move into the 20th century and on to yet another architectural Big Idea, it is worth remembering that Western architecture had now been locked into nostalgia one way or another, ever since the Renaissance. Cities were not celebrated as part of the future, they were simply continuations of the past. The mightiest monuments, from St. Peter's Basilica to the Palace of Versailles, could only look backwards to the supposed glories of former civilisations to find a springboard for their effects. Hard as it may be to accept when we look at some of the stupendous buildings that emerged from such thinking, architecture as a force for genuine urban change had been stagnating for the 500 years that followed the Middle Ages.

This, at any rate, was the view of a new group of architects who came to together at the beginning of the 20th century dissatisfied with an apparently unbreakable insistence on the part of society to maintain literal continuity with the past.

The seeds of dissent had been sown by the iron masters of the 19th century; whatever crimes against aesthetics Eiffel might have been accused of, at least no one criticised his Tower for being old-fashioned. Even so, the contrast between the contemporary appeal of the Paris Opera House and Eiffel's spidery monument was complete. Rich, dense, monumental buildings whose effects were rooted in the past seemed always to be preferred to unfamiliar experiments with the natural materials of the present. From the beginning of the 20th century the architectural avant garde decided that the moment was propitious to cut the ties with

right The Chrysler Building in New York is still the ultimate expression of corporate image, with a machine-age art deco streamlining (and even details based on hub caps!) celebrating the automobile origins of its creation

151

the chrysler building, new york

above Windows and decoration on the Scheepvarthuis, Amsterdam

below Erich Mendelsohn's Einstein Tower in Potsdam, Germany

right Clearly influenced by Cubism, the Town Hall in Hilversum, Holland, designed by Marinus Dudok in 1930

the past forever. One significant practical motivation was the large numbers of office buildings and other commercial, residential, and civic structures that were now increasingly in demand to service a rapidly industrializing society.

Technology and the political events of the new century also primed the climate of change. World War I and the Russian Revolution would be powerful catalysts; Europe's internal organization had changed profoundly and there was growing a widespread appetite for some new, rational sense of order to be established.

Meanwhile a gradual acceptance of the new machine age would further stimulate the appetite for change. This new age, after all, had now provided the influential middle classes with palpably useful gadgets, not just public utilities. Telephones, household appliances and automobiles were becoming available to the better off. Steamships crossed the oceans. Most magical of all was that man's oldest fantasy had come true in the form of aviation.

The image of the machine so fired public imagination that it became a model for explaining many other phenomena – including the workings of the human body. Significantly, Le Corbusier would soon assert that 'the house is a machine for living in'.

There was practical dissatisfaction as well as aesthetic disapproval. It was argued that the use of decorative elements from different architectural periods and styles resulted in hybrid, unorganic buildings whose efficiency was inevitably compromised.

It would soon be time for another Big Idea.

expressionism

That idea would be a movement informally titled the International Style, but preceding it was an interesting if minor 20-year experiment in Northern Europe which, whilst acknowledging the redundancy of historicism and the legitimacy of the new building technologies, nonetheless shared Gaudí's dream of making buildings expressive pieces of large scale sculpture. Whilst they never took things to such Art Nouveau extremes as Gaudí, the Northern European Expressionists still sought to give their buildings the same impact as three-dimensional art.

Expressionism surfaced in art as well, and it was Germany, with its traditional fondness for grand expressive gestures, that stimulated the start of the architectural movement. In fact much Expressionist theory remained just that, with polemics and treatises far outweighing built achievement. However, practising Expressionist artists in Germany included the Russian Vassily Kandinsky, and Franz Marc who produced some of the earliest non-representational art, in a bid to inspire emotion through abstract images rather than figurative depictions. Their work found its architectural echo in the buildings of Erich Mendelsohn, Hans Poelzig and Bruno Taut among others. The most important surviving structure of German expression is Mendelsohn's Einstein Tower outside Potsdam, Germany built between 1920–1. Conceived as an observatory for a research colleague of Albert Einstein, the building is, in its construction, reminiscent of the modern adobe style of New Mexico where the traditional amorphous-looking mud structure is replicated in brick smothered in amorphous concrete. In the case of the Einstein Tower the aim is not to recreate an effect but to evoke some living creature, crouched in the landscape of which it seems almost an organic part. The fact that the observatory is really a regular building with a sculptural layer of concrete on top explains why the interior is rather disappointingly conventional – a charge which could certainly not be made about Hans Poelzig's Grosses Schauspielhaus in Berlin (1918–19). This was to be a 'total theatre' building with decidedly proletarian overtones, in which the structure itself (actually adapted from a circus building) would rival any performance it housed. It became a magic cavern hung with rings of stylised stalactites that, in their regularity, look almost Islamic. In this giddy interior Poelzig demonstrated that Expressionism could be extended from external sculptural effects to invest interiors with the same sort of psychological overtones.

Bruno Taut promoted the new technology to weird levels with his view that glass was some form of spiritual nostrum capable of curing evil in the world. His Glass Pavilion for the glass industry at the Deutscher Werkbund Exhibition of Cologne in 1914 was inscribed with the legend 'Coloured Glass Destroys Hatred', an optimistic view of the human condition, to say the least. The Pavilion itself was of some interest, a glass-faceted, pineapple-shaped dome sitting on a 14-sided glass brick base, animated inside with moving water and coloured facings.

Holland was the other major host to Expressionism between 1915 and 1920, where the work of Hendrik Petrus Berlage, the influential Amsterdam Exchange building, set the tone for the masterwork of Johan van der Mey, Piet Kramer and Michel de Klerk: the Scheepvarthuis,

Cantilevers

A cantilever is a beam supported at only one end. It carries a load at the other end or along its unsupported portion. Cantilevers are used extensively in building – any beam built into a wall with its free end projecting forms a cantilever. The obvious advantage of a cantilever, especially in a large building, is that it allows clear space below, with no columns or other supports to clutter the space; for this reason it can look visually very light, almost as if it is floating. The equally obvious drawback is that the leverage of the load means that a beam supported at only one end needs to be strong to avoid distortion or collapse. Glass and steel, in combination with reinforced concrete, are the most common materials for building cantilevers. Technology was a crucial factor in the development of the International Style. After the experiments of the pioneers of steel-frame building it was now widely recognized that traditional masonry construction was an obsolescent technology. The use of ferro concrete for secondary support elements like floors, and of glass curtain walling meant that modern building had evolved for itself an entirely new of materials. A new generation of architects set about incorporating that palette into an architecture that frankly celebrated its new technical components while seeking individuality through expressive forms, not applied decoration. The supposed result was that the form and appearance of the modern building would declare the materials it was made from and the structural engineering which had brought it about. The ultimate aim was a building style that would blend individual expression, high functionality and an honest utilization of materials

Amsterdam (1912–16). These architects, although technically only authors of the design of the brick façade, became the leading lights of Dutch Expressionism, also known as The Amsterdam School. Interestingly The Amsterdam School was already exploring some of the concerns of the upcoming International Style, in its service of a local spirit of radical socialism which decreed that a decline in the quality of workers' houses must be arrested. The finest works of Kramer and Klerk were therefore not commercial buildings but housing estates commissioned by two socialist housing authorities: Eigen Haard and De Dageraad. Theatrical in their exterior effects – with bold patterns of coloured bricks, oriels, gables and turrets – these workers' homes returned the focus of architectural invention to practical working buildings inhabited by real people.

international style

In the confusing area of architectural labels, 'International Style', 'International Modern' and 'Modernism' are attempts to describe more or less the same thing. The phrase 'International Style' derived from an essay by Henry-Russell Hitchcock and Philip Johnson which appeared as a catalogue for a 1932 architectural exhibition held at the Museum of Modern Art in New York. The exhibition, and the phrase, connoted the architectural style that had developed in Europe and America during the previous decade as a response to the circumstances outlined above.

The essay identified 'a single body of discipline, fixed enough to integrate contemporary style as a reality and yet elastic enough to permit individual interpretation and to encourage natural growth'. Benign but vague, this description did not go quite as far as the mission statement of the European Congrès Internationaux d'Architecture Moderne of four years earlier which had stated firmly that 'It is only from the present that our architectural work should be derived'. Standardization and rationalization were the keys, according to CIAM, and the objective was nothing less than making the everyday urban fabric and form of the town and city the vehicle of good architecture. The housing of ordinary people was to be the medium for excellence. This was to be a social revolution.

The defining characteristics of International Style buildings are open interior spaces, rectilinear forms, light plane surfaces stripped of superficial ornamentation or decoration, and a visually light appearance often brought about by the use of cantilever construction.

Pioneers of International Style

There were four major figures that dominated the development of the International Style – Le Corbusier, Walter Gropius, Mies van der Rohe and Philip Johnson – which is best explored by examining their theories and work. Their preoccupations were certainly similar in spirit, but their actual careers and their work often make their divergences, rather than their similarities, the easier to identify.

notre-dame-du-haut, ronchamp

left   Considered by many to be Le Corbusier's greatest work, the Chapel at Ronchamp (1950–54)

above   The Villa Savoye at Poissy, clearly influenced by Cubism, which Le Corbusier completed in 1929

above right   Le Corbusier in his Paris studio in 1960; he drowned five years later in an accident off the Cote d'Azur

Le Corbusier 1887–1965

Le Corbusier was the pseudonym of Charles-Édouard Jeanneret, a Swiss architect born in 1887 and destined to take the International Style forward by modifying it with a form of sculptural expressionism.

At the age of 30 he went to live in Paris, where as a painter and a writer he became influential on the emergent new style. He published a collection of articles as *Vers une architecture*, the book in which he famously averred that 'a house is a machine for living in'.

One in a long line of architectural theoreticians stretching back to Vitruvius, Le Corbusier was destined to become the most famous and the most influential; among the most well-known of his tracts are *Urbanisme* (1925), *Quand les cathédrales étaient blanches* (1937) and *Propos d'urbanisme* (1946).

In 1922, he showed two pivotal projects in model form, reflecting his approach to city planning. The Citrohan House model (a play on Citröen, known as a car for the masses) embodied the definitions of modern architecture that the architect only later was to codify in his writings: a house should be supported on pillars to open up the ground underneath; it should have an unornamented façade; windows should be in strips to reveal the frame support of the building (a masonry-built house could not support such windows); and an open, split level floor plan.

The Citrohan House interior provided a spatial contrast between open space living quarters and cell-like bedrooms. The accompanying diorama of a surrounding city showed, prophetically, skyscrapers set in greenery.

Le Corbusier advanced these ideas about urban design at the Exposition des Arts Décoratifs in Paris, in 1925 in a little duplex-flat, that contained the architect's own collection of industrially-produced furniture.

His urban aspirations were realised when an industrialist funded the building of a workers' city outside Bordeaux – 40 radical houses based on the Citrohan House. The results so enraged the local people that the local council refused to lay on a water supply, so ensuring the houses stood empty.

Two years later he also built two houses in an experimental residential quarter of Weissenhof at Stuttgart, this time with happier results. But despite this interest in building for the mass population, Le Corbusier built primarily for the wealthy individuals who commissioned individual houses.

More conflicts with the architectural establishment followed, and one of the immediate results was the creation of the Congrès Internationaux d'Architecture Moderne (CIAM), intended to defend progressive architectural values. By 1930 the CIAM had become more focused upon theories of city planning and Le Corbusier, as secretary of the French chapter, helped to establish its views expressed in his 1933 declaration itemizing some of the basic principles of architecture moderne.

During the war years, restricted to theorizing, he developed his concept of harmonic measures that matched architectural elements to the physical stature of human beings. From 1950 onwards Le Corbusier applied it to the design of all his buildings, saying that he wanted then to incorporate a human scale.

Le Corbusier hoped to bring his town planning theories to bear upon the reconstruction of France after World War II, preparing, in 1945 schemes for cities damaged beyond repair. For Saint Dié, destroyed by war, he recommended redistributing its 30,000 inhabitants into five new, highly functional skyscrapers. His proposals were turned down but eventually the French government commissioned him to build a large private housing complex in Marseille. The revolutionary project – the Unité d'Habitation – was a 'vertical community' of 18 storeys. Its 1,800 inhabitants were housed in 23 types of split-level apartment. They shared internal streets, shops, a school and rooftop facilities: nursery, crêche, gym and open-air theatre. It was Completed in 1952, and two similar Unités were built in Nantes and Briey.

These verticle communities set more precedents than one. He saw the social benefits of his ideas, but many who followed saw only the convenience and cheapness of such projects, many of which were hardly communities at all. And despite his belief in social engineering and his impact on a whole generation of architects, Le Corbusier's most famous houses were those of the wealthy, such as the yacht-like Notre-Dame-du-Haut, Ronchamp, the Villa Savoye or the Maisons Jaoul.

Adolph Walter Gropius 1883–1969

Gropius was born in Berlin, Germany, 31 years before the outbreak of World War I. He died in Boston, USA , in the year before the Beatles split up – a telling span of years. During his lifetime architecture and the world changed more than they had ever done before.

Gropius was an architect and educator who greatly influenced the path that modern architecture would take. His buildings, often undertaken as collaborations, included the Harvard University Graduate Center, Cambridge, Massachusetts, and the U.S. Embassy in Athens, Greece.

He had worked in an architectural office in Berlin in 1904 and built his first buildings, farm labourers' cottages in Pomerania two years later. In 1907 he joined the office of the architect Peter Behrens in Berlin, a move which was to influence him profoundly. As well as being a forward-looking architect Behrens was an accomplished industrial designer, a combination of talents that encouraged the 'building as machine perspective'.

After leaving Behrens' office in 1910 Gropius began to develop theories about aligning creative design principles with the opportunities presented by machine production. He championed site assembly of prefabricated parts and asserted that it was up to the designer to bring life to 'the dead product of the machine.'

He then designed two buildings in collaboration with Adolph Meyer: the Fagus Works at Alfeld-an-der-Leine in 1911, and some model industrial buildings in Cologne in 1914, created for an exhibition. The Fagus Works is composed of large areas of glass wall broken by visible steel supports; The Cologne buildings were rather more formally geometric.

Wounded in World War I, Gropius began work again even before the conflict ended, when the city of Weimar consulted him on the future of local art education. In 1919 Gropius became director of two separate schools of art which were immediately combined to form what was to become the world's most

famous academy of art, architecture and design, and which would end two centuries of dominance by the French École des Beaux-Arts. The new academy was called Staatliches Bauhaus Weimar – The Public House of Building Weimar. In fact this school of design, architecture and the applied arts was in existence for just 14 years – 1919 to 1933. It was based in Weimar until 1925, then in Dessau until 1932, and finally in Berlin for a matter of months. In fact the name does not translate easily, Bauhaus is an inversion of the German word Hausbau, describing the process of building a house.

This new 'house of building' placed architecture at the centre of creative activity, making it the reference point for the study of various crafts and other skills.

By training students equally in art and in technically accomplished craftsmanship, Gropius sought to end the traditional schism between the two, so picking up the early concerns of the English designer William Morris who, in the mid-19th century, had

similarly sought to bridge the same gap. Later Morris' efforts led to the Arts and Crafts Movement whose emphasis on individually-made quality objects found no sympathy with Gropius. For him mass production had to be part of any legitimate 20th century design initiative. However Gropius' thinking and the Bauhaus had many other far-reaching influences.

Gropius saw architecture and design as ever changing, always related to the contemporary world. He spoke of the architect's duty to encompass the total visual environment. He himself designed furniture, a railway car and an automobile. He emphasized housing and city planning, the usefulness of sociology, and the necessity of using teams of specialists.

Exiled by the Nazis, to England and then America, throughout his long working life he inspired generations of students at Harvard where he taught and formed an Architects' Collaborative, continuing to work with young colleagues.

the bauhaus

left The spectacular geometry of
the balconies on the building housing
the Bauhaus school and studios

above A view from the ground of
the flat-fronted Bauhaus building

The Bauhaus

The Bauhaus found its definitive home in 1925, six years after it was
founded by Walter Gropius and eight years before it closed for good.
The move came in order to escape from the growing antipathy of the
conservative Weimar community, and it provided Gropius with the
opportunity to design a purpose-made school building and faculty housing
in a less-opinionated industrial town.

The school building was to become a seminal moment in modern
architecture and Gropius' best-known building. Its plan consisted of three
L-shapes radiating from a central point. Each L-shape was systematically
subdivided, with the three outer wings housing workshops, teaching
rooms and – in its sole five-storeyed block.

Variously joined to the centre via an elevated section and a single-
storeyed unit containing a dining room and an auditorium, the flat-roofed
arms of the Bauhaus' studio/dormitories created a dynamic composition
set off with smooth white walls interrupted by flush horizontal ribbon
windows. By undercutting the non-elevated parts of the building with
setback half-basements, Gropius was able to give the building a feeling of
lightness, as if it were floating just above the ground. Seen from the air the
rotary aspect of the design suggested a piece of revolving machinery, a
plane propeller or fan blades. Gropius said that the aerial view was the
principal perspective of his building, a fact not unconnected with industrial
Dessau's being the home of the Junkers aircraft factory.

Ludwig Mies van der Rohe
1886–1969

The work of Mies van der Rohe threatens to impose yet another label on the International Style. 'Miesian' has slipped into the international architectural vocabulary to suggest the elemental simplicity of the style at its purest.

The son of a master mason, van der Rohe helped his father on various construction sites, a practical alternative to the architectural training he never received. In 1905, at the age of 19, he went to work for an architect in Berlin, soon leaving to work instead for a leading furniture designer who favoured the Art Nouveau style.

Two years later van der Rohe received his first commission, a traditional suburban house, of which he made such an accomplished job that Peter Behrens made him an offer of employment which he accepted. At Behrens' office he worked alongside Walter Gropius and Le Corbusier.

Under Behrens influence van der Rohe soon subscribed to the theory of 'a marriage between art and technology' – the same idea that sustained Gropius and laid the foundation of the International Style.

He was also influenced by Hendrik Petrus Berlage, the pioneering Dutch architect whose work – especially the Amsterdam Exchange – fired van der Rohe's own developing enthusiasm for structural honesty which would eventually culminate in totally uncompromising buildings where virtually no structural element was disguised.

In 1919 he designed his revolutionary glass skyscrapers, designs which were to prove of immense influence even though they existed only on paper. In a series of drawings and sketches he proposed The Friedrichstrasse Office, an all steel-and-glass building that established the Miesian principle of minimal frame-and-skin construction.

His Glass Skyscraper design of 1921 explored the idea of a building whose transparent façade actually reveals the steel frame beneath. Both buildings remained unbuilt, but were to prove seminal in the work van der Rohe would do after relocating to Chicago in 1937.

There, as director of the School of Architecture at what would later become the Illinois Institute of Technology, he began a 20-year stay which made the school world-famous, not least for its campus, designed by him between 1939-41.

It was a classic Mies building – simple cubic spaces, exposed structural steel, large areas of glass and brick. All was rational and reasonable to the architect who liked to quote St. Thomas Aquinas, saying 'Reason is the first principle of all human work'.

Later on his American career he was given the opportunity to build his glass skyscrapers, and these

include the Chicago Lake Shore Drive Apartments (1949–51) and the Seagram Building (1956–58) in New York on whose exterior he collaborated with Philip Johnson.

These buildings exemplify Mies's famous principle of 'less is more'. The International Style was reaching its fullest expression around the middle of the 20th century, and van der Rohe had proved to be the most focussed and influential of its many adherents.

Steel-and-glass office buildings influenced by his work appeared all over New York, Chicago and then the United States and the rest of the world. Modern cities, from Singapore to Seattle, would never look the same again.

The Seagram Building

The Seagram Building, New York City, is considered by many to be one of the great buildings of the 20th century. Built in 1958 by Mies van der Rohe and the man who brought him to America, Philip Johnson, it stands in its own plaza, a luxurious skyscraper clad in solid bronze and tinted glass and occupying only a quarter of its prime real estate lot on Park Avenue. The plaza in which the building sits raises it up on a presentational platform and creates a subtly appropriate setting from which to view it and through which to approach it.

A masterpiece of minimalist effects, The Seagram Building looks effortless, although in its precise calculation of every detail and proportion, it is not. Sad proof of this lies all around it, where pale imitations offer mute evidence that an elegant skyscraper cannot be achieved by vague mimicry, only by a full understanding of the volumes and details involved.

right One of the major architectural sights in New York City, the Seagram Building by Mies van der Rohe

the seagram building, new york

The Guggenheim Museum

The Guggenheim Museum (1956–9) is a late example of Frank Lloyd Wright's work. Wright never lost his ability to surprise, and this piece of late Modernism seems at first to owe more to the sci-fi films than to any considered building principle. However, if its external appearance seems bizarre, its internal space must rank with some of Wright's best work. Here was a fluid, natural space in which the viewer could take the elevator to the top and make a languid descent down a spiral ramp, exploring alcoves between the radial piers always with a natural route unwinding in front. The Guggenheim Museum can have some claim to being in the best spirit of the International Style. By rejecting the traditional static, room-by-room display pattern of fine art, it encouraged a fresh approach to viewing exhibits, making what Wright intended to be 'an uninterrupted beautiful symphony' out of the paintings and the building which housed them.

above The elegant spiral ramp of the Guggenheim Museum which achieves a perfect and relaxed way for the visitor to view works of art

right The exterior of the Guggenheim Museum at 1071 Fifth Avenue, New York City

Philip C. Johnson b.1906

Philip Johnson remains something of an enigmatic figure, if such an energetic self-publicist can be called enigmatic. He was one of the original enthusiasts of the International Style, even helping to supply that name, and yet his later career also represented its changing fortunes.

A philosophy major from Harvard, Johnson became director of the Department of Architecture of the Museum of Modern Art in New York in 1932, staging the famous exhibition of International Style and coining its label for the catalogue he wrote with Henry-Russell Hitchcock (although the name was actually proposed by Alfred Barr, then director of MoMA).

Johnson returned to Harvard in 1940 studying architecture with Marcel Breuer. His inspiration, however, was Mies van der Rohe, whom he subsequently brought to New York and with whom he would later collaborate on Seagram Building, New York City.

Johnson's first building was his own house in Cambridge, Massachusetts, in 1942. Finding himself an agreeable client, he then built a second house in New Canaan, Connecticut in 1949, this time a dazzling piece of modernism, much influenced by one of Mies van der

Rohe's houses built four years earlier, but still a dazzling piece of work. A glass prism in parkland, it contains a circular bathroom and reveals Johnson's growing preoccupation with the manipulation of geometric forms. Many more houses followed, as well as the Museum of Modern Art's most elegant garden.

Johnson's tendency to experiment, sometimes quite wildly, led to a clutch of eclectic buildings which included a roofless church in Indiana and a very Beaux-Arts-flavoured New York State Theater, part of the Lincoln Center complex. The Temple Kneses Tifereth Israel, Port Chester, N.Y. (1954–55), marked a change of direction for Johnson as the Miesian influence appeared to decline, arch forms started to appear and historical allusions – anathema to the Modern movement – became more evident. Even so, at more or less the same time he collaborated with his hero van der Rohe on the Seagram Building, a purist International Style Manhattan skyscraper of great elegance and a perfect expression of the values that Johnson had almost single-handedly introduced to America. Even so, Johnson's contributions are largely in the interior, notably the famous Four Seasons Restaurant in the lobby.

His subsequent works include the Pennzoil Place complex in Houston – two dark mirror glass administration towers sandwiching a glass public space – and the now notorious AT&T building in New York City (1977), a skyscraper confection of Art Deco, Renaissance and Neo-Classical references surmounted by a top that mimics a Chippendale cabinet. Johnson, although more playful and ultimately more lightweight in his approach, must still count as one of the International Style's most influential figures. He combines this with offering a link to Post-Modernism, the inevitable reaction against the forward-looking credo, sparse lines, functional appearance and honesty of purpose of the International Stylists.

lever house

above Designed by Phillip Johnson in 1951, Lever House in New York set the style for the glass-and-steel clad skyscraper for years to come

12

post-modernism

& beyond

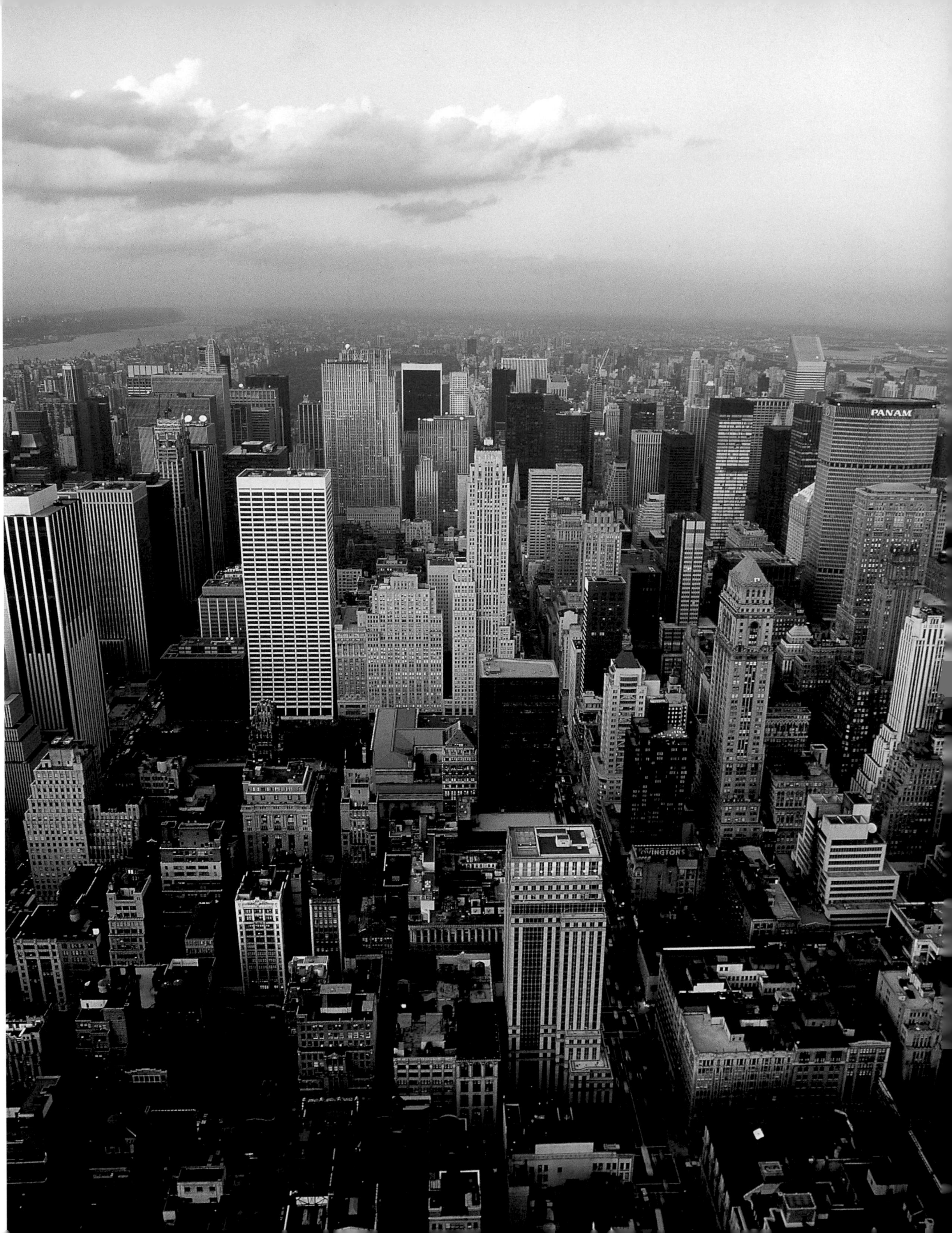
PANAM

a change of direction

In the space of about 30 years or so, many cities the world over had started on a course of great change, immediate or gradual, as a result of what was now usually referred to – rather imprecisely – as the new 'Modern' movement in architecture.

However, no matter what the architectural theorists and practising avant garde architects might believe, for many people living in those cities 'Modern' had become little more than a derogatory adjective suggesting sterile, difficult or self-conscious buildings that lacked the familiarity and charm of the traditional. ('Modern' art was to become a similarly glib label, implying a self-regarding élitist output, suspected of being unskilled and primarily designed to shock or confuse). Does this matter? As we have seen, throughout history any new building experiment usually attracted hostility at first. Architectural thinkers might argue that all innovation at first invites philistinism. However, these same architectural thinkers would have to admit that not only is architecture not art, much of the founding thought of the International Style or Modern movement had been socially benign in its declared aspirations. The people who worked in cities were, at last, to be the ones to benefit from an architecture that would make their home and working environments more enjoyable. It follows that if they did not enjoy them, there was no benefit and no amount of academic argument could change that.

'The only people left trapped in worker housing in America today', wrote Tom Wolfe waspishly in 1981, 'are those who don't work at all and are on welfare'. Wolfe's book *From Bauhaus to Our House* was an unrelenting tirade against what Wolfe saw as the confidence trick pulled by Philip Johnson and his cohorts in bringing to America the profoundly inappropriate social values of post-World War I Germany.

'The United States had not been reduced to smoking rubble by the First World War' he continued. 'She had emerged from the war on top of the world. She was now one of the Great Powers, young, on the rise, bursting with vigor and rude animal health… there was little interest in socialism. There was not even any interest in worker housing… nevertheless it had to be… the great new architectural vision of Worker Housing would have to be brought to America by any means necessary, in any form necessary. Any form.'

Wolfe was articulating – perhaps overstating – what many felt, although he may have been laying at the door of some genuine pioneers blame that ought to have been directed at inferior imitators. Even so, the sterile canyon of New York City's 6th Avenue's towering glass skyscrapers – certainly more bad ones than good ones – does somehow fail to capture the spirit of the city quite as well as does the Chrysler Building – ridiculous but still fresh and charming – or even the Empire State Building, a cliché that refuses to go out of fashion. Ornament had given way to sheer glass walls and to concrete – which soon proved itself to be an unappealing material for external finishes anywhere other than in Mediterranean countries. Weather staining was inevitable, ugly and irreversible. On a practical level, hermetically sealed office buildings proved impossible to ventilate without expensive air-conditioning systems.

left New York's Manhattan, the world's most famous skyline and the epitome of 20th century modern

Undeniably there was a continuing popular resistance to many of the expressions of Modernism which were frequently seen as dehumanizing and joyless alternatives to the decorative and allusive architectural adventures of the past. Architects taking this on board began to look for new ways to reflect what, by the 1960s, was already becoming a world fast-changing in social attitudes, and, very soon, in technological complexion as well.

above Robert Venturi with his model for the extension to the National Gallery in London, the Sainsbury Wing

the rise of the urban theorists

The supposed failings of the Modern movement, particularly in North America, were the subject of two highly influential books in the 1960s.

The first was Jane Jacobs' *The Death and Life of Great American Cities* published in 1961. In it she maintained that cities had been rendered incoherent by the inappropriate application of the theories of the International Style. The practice of breaking with the past as a point of doctrinaire principle and starting afresh had robbed American cities of their natural sense of order and space, she argued.

Certainly if we think back to the archetypal Muslim urban space, where incremental organic growth defined everything, there are few parallels to be found in those Western cities of the mid-20th century upon which utopian, tradition-less modern plans have been imposed.

The second book, published five years later, was Robert Venturi's *Complexity and Contradiction in Architecture*. The book was academic and at times difficult, but its central message was clear enough.

'Less is not more' he said, evoking the Miesian central tenet of International Style, 'Less is a bore'.

Venturi went on to state his argument that a building reduced to puritanical geometric shapes lacked the valuable referential quality of historical architecture. He maintained that, without references and quotations, buildings became effete and lacked any associations or ironic touches. Architecture, he argued, should be hybrid, not pure, inclusive, not exclusive. He applauded the 'messy vitality' of the great architecture of the past, arguing that it surpassed the functional steel-and-glass boxes of the International Style.

Venturi's manifesto had a great impact on a new generation of architects who were beginning to experience similar problems with the Modernist legacy.

The demolition of several 14-storey slab blocks that had been built as part of the award-winning Pruitt-Igoe housing development in St. Louis, Missouri, only 20 years earlier and based on designs by Minoru Yamasaki, marked the start of a reaction against Modernism. Yamasaki had been thought of as one of the kinder spirits of the Modern movement (he was also the architect of New York's World Trade Center) and so the demolition took on potent symbolic meaning for the architectural community.

The St. Louis offensive also signalled the start of a similar demolition programme later pursued in Europe as well as America as 'vertical communities' were decried, razed and replaced with more familiar horizontal ones.

above After much controversy, the Sainsbury Wing at the National Gallery echoed classicism and in doing so satisfied traditionalists

right The celebrated AT&T Building in New York City with its familiar Chippendale finish, a monument to postmodernist populism

What is remarkable about Venturi's influence is that he was at the time almost exclusively a theoretician. His book, and that of Jane Jacobs, gave rise to a movement based on very little but theory. Venturi had studied at the Princeton University School of Architecture and worked for Eero Saarinen (in Bloomfield Hills, Michigan), and Louis I. Kahn (in Philadelphia), before launching his own firm with John Rauch in 1964.

Even so, he could at the time claim little in the way of built achievement: Post-Modernism (sometimes called Second Modernism) was in the main based upon the musings of dissatisfied intellectuals and further encouraged by the various grumblings of dissatisfied critics and consumers.

In 1967 Venturi's wife, Denise Scott Brown, became a partner in his firm and in 1972 co-authored *Learning from Las Vegas* with Venturi and Steven Izenour. Here the anti-Modernist argument went further, taking as its extreme model the Nevada desert gambling town whose neon-lit urban sprawl and the car-oriented urban architecture was the precise opposite of all the Modernists held dear but which offered Venturi and his co-authors aromatic food for thought.

Roadside billboards, signs and symbols, neon vistas and electric-hued interiors complete with kitsch statuary and electronic gadgetry, infact all the ephemera surrounding modern architecture, seemed to Venturi to be 'the forgotten symbolism of architectural form'.

When Venturi did build he sought to promote the concerns of mass culture to the realm of high art. Turning to historical precedent in his later work, he favoured the 19th-century Shingle style of domestic architecture. He also designed the Humanities Classroom Building of the State University of New York at Purchase, USA (1973) and the Franklin Court, Independence National Historical Park, Philadelphia, USA (1976); these buildings remain difficult to assess without thinking of Venturi's strongly-stated opinions which the buildings seem designed to illustrate and which seem likely to remain Venturi's major achievement.

At the end of the 80s Venturi profited from a famous dispute over the winning design (by Ahrends, Burton & Koralek) of a competition for a new wing to The National Gallery in London's Trafalgar Square. After the Prince of Wales, in a flood of publicity, famously criticized ABK's scheme it was scrapped and eventually Venturi, Rauch & Scott Brown were appointed. The resulting extension, The Sainsbury Wing, was a typically playful and ambiguous commentary on the relevance of classical language to a modern art gallery.

Many American architects in the 1970s and 1980s adopted a version of what Venturi had recommended, and so assisted in creating a kind of populist language scattered with playful classical quotations. Philip Johnson and his partner John Burgee produced the famous New York AT&T Building with its Chippendale memento.

Many other so-called Postmodernist architects had of course started out on their careers embracing the Modernist creed, and many subsequently persisted in carrying some of this baggage with them into the arena of their conversion. Two prime examples were Michael Graves and Richard Meier .

Michael Graves b. 1934

Born in 1934, Michael Graves was one of the principal figures of the Postmodernist movement. He trained at the University of Cincinnati and at Harvard University, and afterwards studied in Rome from 1960 to 1962 before starting to teach at Princeton University where he became a full professor in 1972.

Graves began his building career in the 1960s as a creator of private houses in the austere style of Modernism. At this point he was clearly an admirer of the pioneers of the International Style, most notably of Le Corbusier. However, like others before him Graves by the late 1970s had found that the cool reductionism of the International Style continued to alienate many people; in response he began to pursue richer effects that any pure Modernists would never consider.

By the early 1980s he had been commissioned to do several large public buildings of which the Portland Public Service Building in Portland, Oregon, USA (1980–83) stands out both for its scale and for the extremity of Graves' treatment. Now definitely the ex-Modernist, he reworked classical elements such as colonnades and loggias in a boldly stylized way that was almost cartoon-like. Initially the building suggests nothing more complex than a child's colourful building block construction, but closer examination reveals a complex layering of subversions and re-inventions of classical elements that could never be mistaken for untutored construction or, indeed, for nostalgia. The building also makes a very direct appeal to the public it is meant to serve with a friendly 'face' suggested by the stylized plasters and keystones of the façade.

The Portland building finds an echo in a famous work by Charles Moore in New Orleans, Louisiana. His Piazza d'Italia, (1975–1980) was intended as a social focus for the Italian community of the city, but instead of taking the traditional American Southern route of replicating the grandeurs of Europe to scale (as for example in Nashville, Tennessee, self-styled 'Athens of The South' and home to a Parthenon clone complete with giant statue of Athena) Moore created a permanent stage set with what look almost like theatrical 'flats' mounted in a curved stage set with an irregular pool. Such structures are obviously intended to reassure the public that modern architecture can be comprehensible and enjoyable; they also implicitly pose the question of why the public should have thought otherwise in the first place.

left The Public Service Building in Portland, Oregon, designed by Michael Graves and built 1980-83

below Richard Meier outside the Guggenheim Museum in 1984, just after receiving the $100,000 Pritzker Prize for Architecture

right An interior of the Neue Staatsgalerie in Stuttgart, Germany, by Sir James Stirling

Richard Meier b. 1934

Whether Richard Meier can be classed as a Postmodernist remains something of a moot point. Less inclined towards the theatrical, he has still wrought some sophisticated changes upon the classic Modernist principles of his early work and he represents another strand in the complex development of Modernism into other things.

Meier was educated at Cornell University, Ithaca, NY, working to begin with for the firm of Skidmore, Owings and Merrill in New York City, and then for Marcel Breuer, the also in New York City and a noted exponent of the International Style.

Meier built his own reputation with a series of dramatic private houses which typically favoured sharply intersecting planes and clean geometric white surfaces. Meier continues to favour the symbolic white of the International Style, declaring 'White is the ephemeral emblem of perpetual movement', another of those boldly meaningless statements with which architects occasionally feel impelled to undermine their own credibility.

Meier, however, remains much admired by those individuals who tended to be in agreement with Venturi's general premise but find exercises like Michael Graves' Portland Public Services Building a little too hard to take.

Richard Meier's designs for the Museum of Modern Art in Florence, Italy (1974), and the Bronx Developmental Center in New York (1976) both reflected his continuing concern with the way that public and private spaces interact within the context of the city.

the city in time

The development of The City in the 20th century has been a process of extraordinary vitality. Often cities have changed so fast as to leave behind all traditional notions of shape, boundary and identity. Los Angeles is often described as six suburbs in search of a city, a lethally accurate gibe that obliges us to reconsider the forces which shape modern cities.

In Britain, house prices in the city of York escalated when the railway service to London cut the journey time to less than two hours. York, 200 miles away, was now within daily commuting distance of the capital. This apparent nonsense was perhaps a legitimate perception in a world where it might take a commuter two hours to get to central London by road even if he lived in a suburb only 25 miles away. The geographically accurate map of the city – any city – is likely to be the one of least practical use to us now. The classic map of London's complex underground railway system, designed in the 1930s, presaged today's urban needs by depicting stations not where they were but entirely schematically in terms of how they related to one another.

Early morning TV bulletins about weather, traffic and rail services are now part of city life: electronic information is of far more use to us in negotiating the city than actually going out there and taking a look.

Affordable personal computers and global communications mean that traditional workplaces are unlikely to survive: often there is simply no need

Sir James Stirling 1926–1992

Born in Glasgow, Scotland, the son of a marine engineer, James Stirling was another architect who came to Postmodernism gradually. After training at the University of Liverpool's School of Architecture, Stirling began his career with some radical designs for public buildings and multi-unit housing in the 1950s,

His early schemes were low-rise-housing projects that flaunted their rough steel and brick components in the best traditions of Modernist honesty; a notable example is a complex of flats at Ham Common (1955–8) done when he was in partnership with James Gowan. The same partnership produced the Engineering Department building for the University of Leicester (1959–63) which was perhaps Stirling's most important and best-known contribution in this idiom.

After splitting with Gowan in 1963, Stirling began to flirt with Postmodernism using colourful decoration elements and complex geometric shapes. More housing, this

time in Runcorn, England, (1967–76) reflected this playfulness with its building block forms and porthole-style windows.

From 1971 he was in partnership with Michael Wilford and this alliance produced Stirling's most famous and most widely admired building: the Neue Staatsgalerie (1977–84), in Stuttgart, Germany, a combination of classicism and Postmodern abstraction. Among his other works are a new building for the Fogg Museum (1979-84) and the Arthur M. Sackler Museum (1985), both at Harvard University. Also in the 80s Stirling was responsible for the Tate Gallery outpost at Albert Dock, Liverpool, England, which led to one of his most overtly Postmodern schemes, with his fondness for marine imagery this time finding a more natural home.

to arrange a city along traditional lines. Already the populations of many major cities in the West are falling as people move out of town.

Old cities often find it hard to adapt their infrastructure. New cities in the world's new economic regions are able to start from scratch. Singapore was able to turn its small city/ Republic into a highly sophisticated wired environment, a fully cabled city. It also built itself a dazzlingly prestigious underground railway system at colossal expense because it was perceived as a status symbol. New York and London have larger underground systems variously antiquated, noisy, hostile and inefficient. They cannot be rebuilt from scratch without involving colossal investment and unacceptable levels of disruption.

Ask middle class inner city dwellers their views on the city they live in and building design will be low on their list of concerns if it appears at all: their answers are likely to centre on issues like crime, traffic congestion, pollution, education and public transport.

What is the common strand of all these things? It is that none of them have much to do with architecture, at least in direct terms. Town planning and local governmental issues dominate. Even so, ironically, architecture still arouses great passions. Although architecture is no longer popularly seen as the direct key to unlocking the solutions to civilised cities, the way buildings look and feel is still a subject of genuine concern and often acrimonious debate.

So has the 20th century architectural debate been reduced to a simple two-team contest of traditionalists versus modernists?

other paths

In truth Postmodernism is just another unsatisfactory label, at least judging by the variety of buildings that it has been used to identify. There is certainly a considerable degree of pluralism in the varied responses to the decline of Modernism and the experiments to find an architecture to match the times.

Popular Postmodernism was typified in Britain by Terry Farrell who in 1983 designed TV-am Studios, Camden Town, London (purpose-built for Britain's pioneer breakfast television company) a building featuring giant eggs in eggcups and similar external references that could hardly be accused of being difficult or obscure. A decade later, and more surprisingly, Farrell was commissioned to design the new building that would house a British intelligence service on the South Bank of the Thames at Vauxhall, London. This too took an approach closer to Michael Graves' Portland building than any traditional notion of what security headquarters might look like. Still in Britain Nicholas Grimshaw meanwhile pursued architectural forms popularly referred to as High-Tech because of their machine-like appearance. A stone's throw from Farrell's playful TV-am building is an 80s complex by Grimshaw that combines a supermarket with a series of pod-like residential units, an exact expression of the house as 'a machine for living in'.

At the same time in Britain Quinlan Terry pursued unreconstructed classical renewal at his Riverside Development, Richmond, England (1986-88), as did John Simpson at Ashfold House, Sussex, England (1985-87). The same traditional approach was taken up sporadically in France, witnessed by Christian Langlois' Senate Building, rue de Vaugirard, Paris (1975), and Regional Council Building in Orléans (1979-81).

Flying the British flag for overt technology has been Sir Richard Rogers who, with Renzo Piano created the famous Centre Pompidou, Paris (1971-77), with its services and structure not only exposed externally but converted into unmissable features through bright primary coloration. Truthful exposure of the structural bones of a building or Postmodern joke? Either way Richard Rogers revisited the idea in his Lloyd's Building, London (1984-86), a spectacular building which proved another touchstone for architectural debate, especially when its interior was so roundly criticised by those who had to work in it that another firm was eventually called in to rationalise the working spaces.

Yet another variation came with the so-called Neorationalist or elementalist approach that began in Italy when in 1966 architect Aldo Rossi published an influential book, *L'architettura della città* proposing a modulation of classical ideas through the features of the local context in which a building is sited. Among those who subscribed to Rossi's approach were Bruno Reichlin and Fabio Reinhart, whose Casa Tonini, Torricella (1972-74) takes a Palladian model, reduces it to the bare minimum and executes it in pure white concrete. The German architect Oswald Matthias Ungers explored the same kind of rationalist contextualism in Germany, his Stadtloggia in the Hildesheim marketplace (1980) being a good example of this solution to the problem of inserting a new town building into a location already strongly defined by its existing buildings.

below Another London landmark by Terry Farrell, the imposing MI5 (security services) Building in Vauxhall, built in the early 1990s

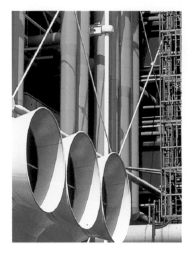

above A detail from the 'inside out' exterior of the Pompidou Centre, Paris, designed by Richard Rogers

below Making the most of the effect of light on his materials, a detail from Rogers' Lloyd's Building

right More 'nuts and bolts' on display, Rogers repeats his Pompidou idea in the City of London, at Lloyd's

The city buildings of Belgian architect Rob also reflect this approach, witness his housing in the Ritterbergstrasse, Berlin (1978–80).

In the 70s the American experimental studio of S.I.T.E. (an acronym for Sculpture In The Environment) headed by James Wines pulled off a memorable coup by persuading the art-collecting owner of a chain of stores to let S.I.T.E. rework the traditional shoe-box type store building usually to be found in the more obscure parts of the American rural landscape. Thus was born a series of playful buildings of which the most famous is the Tilt Showroom of Best Products in Towson, Maryland (1976-8). Here the whole façade seems to be in the process of being pulled open by an invisible giant hand – shades of Venturi's *Learning From Las Vegas* here executed with skill and subtlety to match the wit.

In Japan, Isozaki Arata and Yamashita Kazumasa spearheaded a move towards the postmodernism of Michael Graves and Charles Moore.

Yamashita's Japan Folk Arts Museum, Tokyo (1982) and Isozaki's Fujimi Country Club, Oita, Japan (1973–4) show how wholeheartedly the concept has been imported by a country with a very different building tradition.

In India, Charles Correa abandoned his early adherence to the International style, exemplified by his white concrete hotel at Ahmadabad of the 50s, and in later low-rise housing projects advocated a return to more indigenous building types.

Back in Britain another of the architects more or less contemporary with Farrell, Stirling and Rogers pursued a body of work that comes as close as any to combining an authentic personal vision with a legitimate use of materials whilst remaining separate from Postmodernism, Neorationalism or any other self-conscious reaction against the International Style. In a profession that loves labels, Norman Foster would, however, inevitably be labelled High Tech.

the lloyds building, london

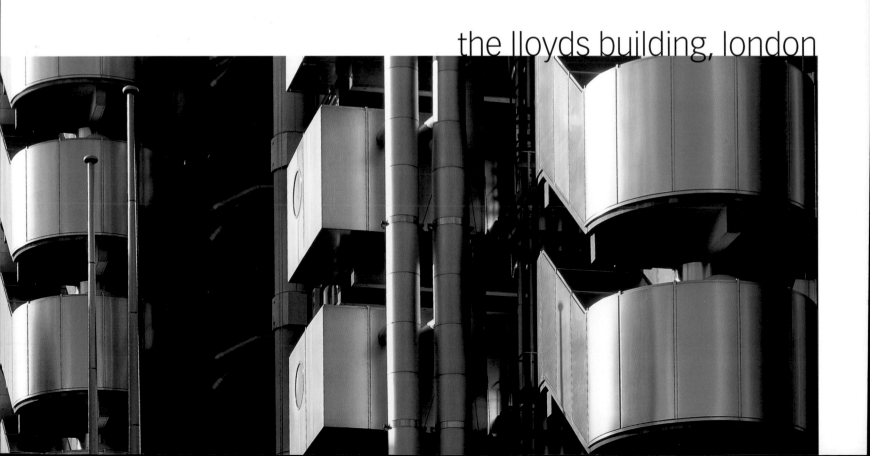

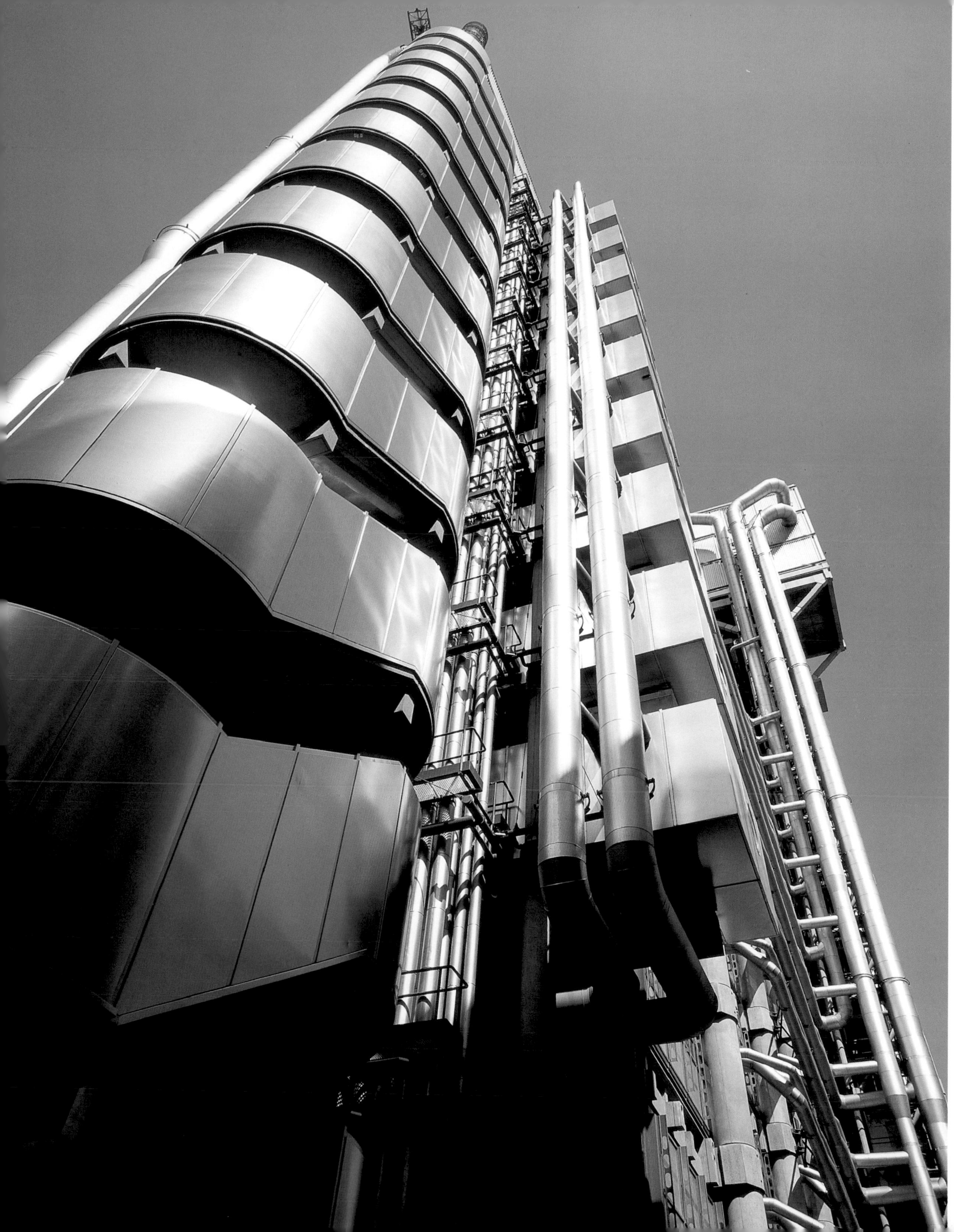

willis faber dumas building

Willis Faber Dumas Building

Rather than advertising its allegiance to this or that stylistic approach, the Willis Faber Dumas building concerned itself solely with solving the problems it was faced with. The result was an extraordinary building.

Given a weirdly irregular, curving site, Foster decided to use all of it and so reduced the height of the building to three storeys. A conventional rectangular plan would have been significantly smaller and required a much higher building to achieve the same internal square footage; this increased height would have made it less welcome in the context of the low rise old town.

The decision to enclose the building entirely with an undulating glass curtain wall involved exceptionally precise calculations and was to prove a quantum leap in the architectural use of glass.

Le Corbusier's proposition of always recreating the building's site on its roof in the form of a garden was here taken quite literally. The result was not only increased leisure space for Willis Faber Dumas staff but one of the best natural insulating materials available – growing turf – which not only reduced running costs but proved so efficient that it eliminated the need for any expansion joints in the structure.

Natural light was admitted centrally over the escalators to enhance the sense of space and freedom; meanwhile the choice of escalators – as opposed to the more common elevators – was a conscious one, taken to encourage staff to continue conversations whilst moving through the building. Elevators, Foster noted, are inclined to silence or constrain social interraction and discourse.

Servicing the office floors was designed for long-term flexibility and the decision to install raised floors throughout – by no means an automatic choice in the mid-70s – paid enormous dividends when soon afterwards wholesale computer cabling became necessary and could be accommodated without major disruption.

The major external feature of the building was its dark glass wall, a sinuous enclosure which in the day presented a mirror surface to reflect neighbouring buildings, so integrating its own bulk unobtrusively into the townscape. At night, as internal lighting overtook external daylight, the building gradually became transparent – a luminous presence that revealed its workings, structural and operational, in an entirely natural way.

Willis Faber Dumas proved a thoughtful building in many ways. It offset the apparent disadvantage of so much glass (glass being an energy wasteful material) because such a deep-plan building had a very low ratio of glass to internal volume. Many of its costs were low because of the economies of scale when ordering such large amounts. For example, 40 miles of aluminium channel was required for the ceiling of just one floor.

Foster would go on to create other major buildings throughout the world, but none has so far had quite the significance or longevity of the Willis Faber Dumas.

above left The entrance elevation of Willis Faber Dumas at night

below left Daytime front elevation

Sir Norman Foster b.1935

Norman Foster began his career as an architect in partnership with Richard Rogers. Together with their wives, Wendy and Su, they set up in London as Team 4, a firm which became Foster Associates in 1967. Given the marked difference between the subsequent work of Foster and Rogers, the early alliance may seem surprising in retrospect, because Foster was soon to establish a fondness for a dominant building type that he has succeeded in reinventing with imagination and authority for thirty years: the large neutral space envelope that lends itself to a multiplicity of uses.

Quite early on Foster established a way of celebrating modern technological materials without turning them into self-conscious monuments or using them ostentatiously. Foster's buildings are frequently distinguished by effortlessly beautiful components that have been developed with rigorous attention to performance and perfection. They recall elements of gliders, fine bicycles and the best industrial design from several fields.

In 1975 Foster Associates built headquarters for an insurance company called (at the time) Willis Faber Dumas in Ipswich, England. The awkward, irregular site set in a loop of roads in an old town with some interesting traditional buildings nearby, the new headquarters could easily have been one of the many forgotten office buildings of the 70s. Instead it was nothing less than a triumph, winning awards, drawing visitors from all over the world, and delivering substantial financial benefits to its owners as well as very high-quality working conditions for its staff. Foster's output after Willis Faber Dumas continued to maintain generally high standards. The Sainsbury Centre For The Visual Arts at the University of East Anglia, England, was perhaps one of the purest examples of the high-tech shed managing to look visually light and elegant whilst housing quite complex but flexible internal spaces. The Hong Kong & Shanghai Bank headquarters building in Hong Kong became a famous landmark, and was more or less single-handedly responsible for a rush of competitive high rise office building there. Of the numerous projects that followed, one of the best has been Stansted Airport, England, a new airport building of considerable elegance. Another building that glows in the dark, Stansted consists of a translucent canopy supported on tree-shaped columns that ensure ample free space beneath. A simple two-level arrival and departure scheme creates an airport that, freed of the clutter of the usual extensions and accretions, shows how rational such buildings can be if designed as a whole from the blank canvas.

Foster's use of materials made possible by new technology – treated glass, insulated panels, strong and light alloy fittings and extrusions, silicons, clamps and bearings – is one legitimate course for contemporary architecture, free from the tug-of-war between nostalgia and stark modernity. While not alone in taking this stance, Foster has been its staunchest advocate for more than three decades, and one of its most dependable exponents.

the city in future

Second-guessing the future is a diverting parlour game almost guaranteed to prove inaccurate – witness some of yesterday's attempts noted in the next chapter. Are we in a position to anticipate what will happen to our cities now that technology is changing the world we live in faster than at any time before?

We may speculate on millennial developments insofar as 'traditional', Postmodernism and High-Tech architecture all look set to continue in some form beyond the year 2000. This, though, may not be the most pressing question when it comes to the shape and character of the cities of tomorrow.

As suggested earlier, whilst architecture will certainly continue to be a most vital force, it may not necessarily be the force that fashions cities in the way it once did.

When cities were relatively stable in shape or form – when even radical change amounted to no more than extending city walls or building new neighbourhoods or monuments – architecture and planning together delineated the spaces and gave them meaning.

The changes already in progress in many of our cities are not of this order. Japan has already experimented with exploiting the benefits of sophisticated digital communications to send workers home to work. Anyone who has ever sat in a rush hour traffic jam in Tokyo or Osaka will know why the alternative of the automated home office appealed. However, it was quickly discovered that in a highly structured society like Japan's, this created intolerable pressures in the home which was never intended to be used this way. As a result experiments have been proposed whereby 'half-way house' offices – located neither in the residential suburbs nor the clogged city centre – equipped with a full range of communications facilities can become the new workplace, staying in touch with the city centre main offices. Strictly speaking unnecessary, but socially desirable, such work centres would create new and (in the traditional sense) quite meaningless satellite cities. Japan too has proposed, and in some cases implemented, a totally new building type: the hotel which is designed to cater for businessmen seeking in equal parts a leisure environment and a full complement of office facilities.

Meanwhile the promise of the intelligent building beckons, promising office buildings with sophisticated computer-controlled internal climates, light- and heat-responsive window laminates and new levels of integrated information gathering and distribution. Satellite conferencing and the rapidly expanding Internet will further modify the concept of business travel. Traditional cities, depleted by vast out of town shopping facilities and an ebbing residential middle class will surely have to re-invent themselves if they are not to implode or become so socially imbalanced as to become conglomerates of ghettos.

Architecture will certainly have a role to play in whatever measures are taken to revamp the urban fabric, but it will not be the prime force. Just as the architect, once the ringmaster of the building design process, has gradually relinquished control to an ever-expanding team of specialists (each of whom knows so much that for one man to know it would be

above A corner detail from Norman Foster's Stansted Airport project showing clearly the canopy supports allowing for free movement below

left Foster's Hong Kong & Shanghai Bank building, a Hong Kong landmark

stansted airport, england

impossible), so too must architecture take its appropriate place in an increasingly complex urban planning process.

There is no need to regret this. Nothing will ever replace the impact of a great building, well-realised in the right context. Architecture is so much a part of the psychological impact of what cities are that it can exist even when the city in question may not; proposed cities, possible cities, fantasy cities, lost cities, fictional cities – none can exist without its architecture. Accordingly the next and final chapter, in place of a more specific and surely doomed prediction of exactly what tomorrow's cities will look like, you will find a collection of urban pipe dreams, some seriously intended, some absurd, some actual proposals, some self-confessed fictions. The only thing they all have in common is that they do not exist. This, if you think about it, makes what they propose more intriguing, not less.

above Glowing in the dark, the transluscent canopy of the Stansted Airport terminal at night

13

parallel universes

in search of utopia

Different building types are established not by architects but by society – or so conventional wisdom goes. Society sets the programme and, through some agency or other, private or public, it hires the architect to find ways and means of achieving them.

This established view of the architect as the skilled provider of a building design service, speaking only when he is spoken to, is not one that has ever found much favour with ambitious architects.

Many architects like to build monuments, preferably to themselves. Some architects see themselves as artists, social engineers or visionaries. Others, railing against their role as servants of the establishment, become theoreticians – authors of myriad 'what if' scenarios with which they may hope to influence the establishment, so that they commission what they themselves want to supply; often though their proposals are so intentionally radical that their objective seems to be to ensure that they remain at the leading edge of theory, perennially influential and permanently unemployable.

On the other hand, very occasionally and when the moment is right, a well-articulated theory can galvanize enough people to prompt almost immediate built investment in its principles. Robert Venturi achieved this, giving Postmodernism its rationale and its opportunity through his writings. More usually, however, architectural theorists cast themselves as outsiders by proposing extreme and mould-breaking ways of looking at cities and buildings. There is a well-founded suspicion that Le Corbusier was himself one of these outsiders, never happier than when he was being rejected by the establishment for his radical theories, and somehow gloomily dissatisfied with the reverence and acceptance he was afforded in later life. His radical *Plan Voisin*, a skyscraper-dominated proposal for the redevelopment of Paris conceived in 1925, went some way towards sustaining his maverick status.

Radical architectural theory, like all architectural theory remains fantasy until it is built. It may be fantasy with a clear social objective; it may be fantasy for its own sake or simply the fantasy of recreating the lost cities of yesterday through imaginative computer modeling, but it remains an illusion, an architecture rooted in the imagination.

In the 18th century Giovanni Battista Piranesi, architect, printmaker and theorist, developed a large body of engravings showing the buildings of ancient Rome in such persuasive detail that they were inspirational in bringing about the Neoclassical movement in art.

His series *Carceri* (Prisons) of about 1745 depicts ancient Roman or Baroque ruins converted into fantastic and ominous futuristic dungeons filled with outlandish scaffolding. Piranesi's exceptionally precise vision, combined with his technical mastery, made his fantasy architecture a precursor of that of the cinema, based as it was upon the seduction of imagery as much as the persuasion of ideas.

Also in the 18th century, Étienne-Louis Boullée, French visionary architect and theorist, created many conceptual designs for public monuments, seeking to elevate the viewer through architectural forms suggestive of the sublime power of nature and of God.

Boullée's late theoretical work was an attempt to distil the essence of ancient architecture into a new, geometrically reduced concept of monumental building that might retain the timeless appeal of classical forms. In his 1784 design *Cénotaphe à Newton* – a giant hollow globe conceived to honour the British physicist – Boullée gave imaginary form to his theories. He was fond of cloaking his fantasy structures in mystery, sometimes showing them partly buried, as though the illusion of unearthing them added extra credibility. Despite a certain overbearing grandiosity, Boullée, in his wish to invent an architectural language appropriate to new idealized social order, did anticipate some of the concerns of 20th-century architecture.

In America in the 1920s, architectural renderer Hugh Ferriss, who had helped to popularize the stepped skyscraper building form through his drawings, took the next logical step and proposed a graphical hypothesis of his own idea of a metropolis for the year 1979.

Between 1912 and 1914 Antonio Sant'Elia made many highly imaginative drawings and plans for cities of the future. Sant'Elia was an Italian socialist who proposed a clean break with the architectural styles of the past and traditional solutions to urban design. His collection of Utopian drawings called *Città Nuova* was exhibited in 1914 at an exhibition of the

left Étienne-Louis Boullée's futuristic design (in 1784) for a Cenotaph dedicated to Sir Isaac Newton

right Cities of the future have abounded in 20th century popular culture, in movie sets, comic books and sci-fi magazine illustration

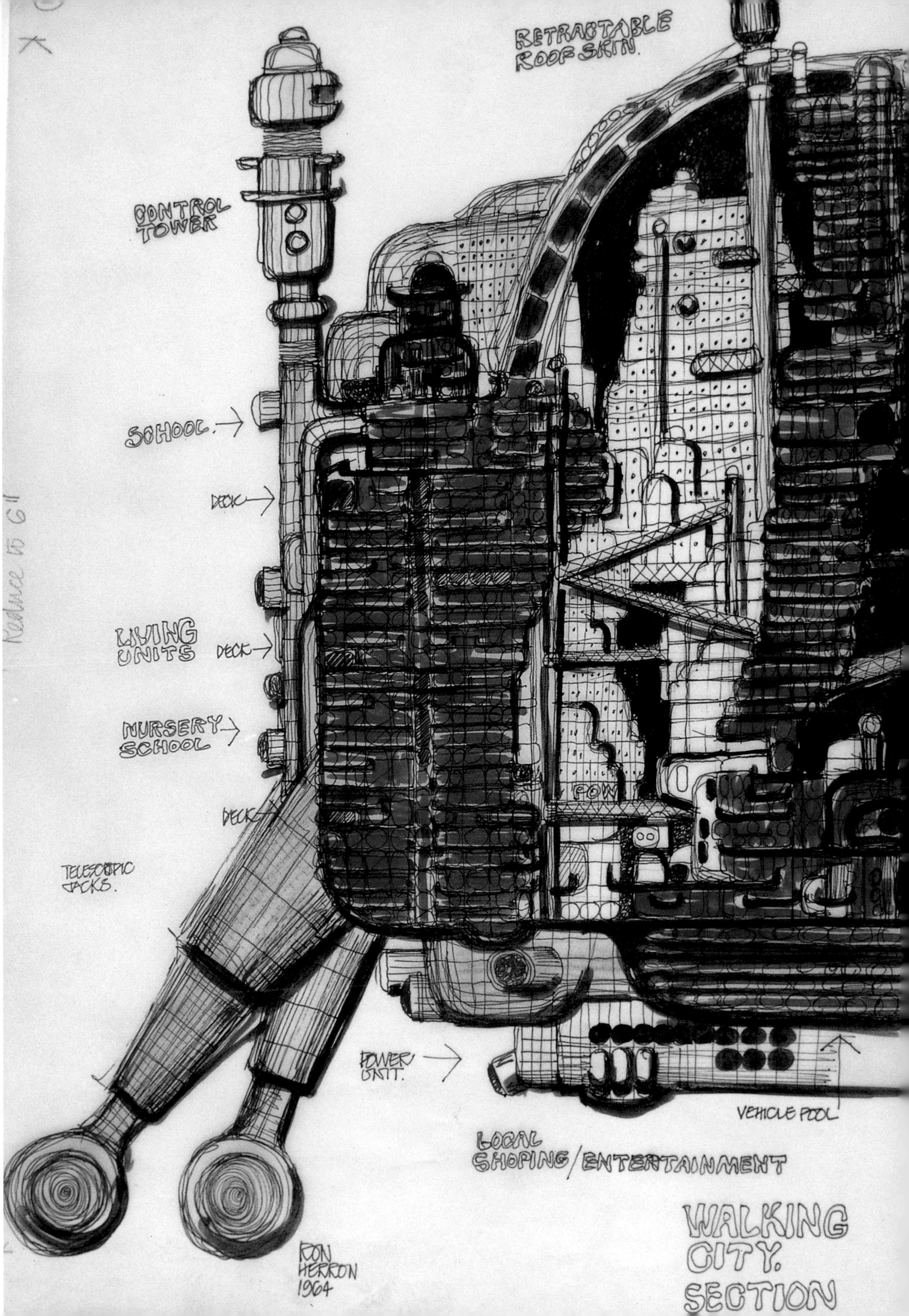

Reduce to 6"

CONTROL
TOWER

RETRACTABLE
ROOF SKIN.

SCHOOL. →

DECK →

LIVING
UNITS

DECK →

NURSERY
SCHOOL →

DECK →

TELESCOPIC
JACKS.

POWER
UNIT. →

VEHICLE POOL

LOCAL
SHOPING/ENTERTAINMENT

RON
HERRON
1964

WALKING
CITY.
SECTION

Nuove Tendenze group to which he belonged. The drawings' chief characteristic was that, in common with Utopian proposals in general, they intentionally espoused a world unconnected to any recognisable present; here a highly mechanized and industrialized city is dotted with skyscrapers and improbable multilevel traffic circulation.

Christopher Alexander, who became Professor of Architecture at the University of California in Berkeley, has made a career out of his elaborate planning theories based upon his studies of original native cultures that have developed unselfconsciously over long periods of time. Alexander argues that by analyzing these processes, ascribing to them mathematical values and then extrapolating findings into other planning scenarios, some form of automatically validated planning system might evolve.

Paolo Soleri, an American architect and designer born in Italy 1919, became a famous utopian city planner after working for Frank Lloyd Wright in Arizona from 1947 to 1949. After returning to Italy for a time he returned to the USA and finally settled Scottsdale, Arizona. The desert milieu dominated his thinking, providing its own image for the vertical community concept. Soleri's *Mesa City* (1959) was the prototype – a desert city capable of housing two million people. Soleri later proposed a series of enormous urban centres extending vertically into space that were intended to conserve the natural surroundings by condensing human life into these integrated environments.

Soleri dubbed his utopian conurbations the product of 'arcology', a word he derived from his twin concerns of 'architecture' and 'ecology'. Soleri was neither the first nor the last to give somewhat bizarre ideas credibility by means of beautiful drawings and models. A 1970 travelling exhibition of these brought him wide publicity in America as did a publication, *Soleri's Arcology: The City in the Image of Man* (1969).

Archigram

Of particular interest was the theoretical work of six young London architects who came together in the early 1960s and shared – some might say even helped define – the spirit of that decade. They met when working for the construction company that was redeveloping London's Euston Railway station (a process that coincided with the disappearance of the Euston Arch, a lost structure which has since become something of a Holy Grail for traditionally-minded architects). They were Peter Cook, Dennis Crompton, Warren Chalk, David Greene, Michael Webb and Ron Herron. To begin with Archigram was the name of their publication, then it became the name of the group which proposed a simple modus operandi: architecture by drawing.

Archigram were lateral thinkers, free-associators, out to break the tyrannical hold of the traditional city by dragooning new technology (some of it not yet quite invented or, in some cases, inventable) and space hardware to expand the possibilities of urban living through disposable elements, moving buildings and many other iconoclastic ideas. As with Piranesi, the key was again the persuasive quality if the draughtsmanship which rendered and publicized these ideas, a key one of which was the notion of the expendable building.

below Ron Herron's fabulous walking city, conceived by the Archigram group in 1964

left A detail of the walking city, with retractable roof skin, schools, living units, shopping and entertainment areas all clearly indicated

EACH WALKING UNIT HOUSES NOT ONLY A KEY ELEMENT OF THE CAPITAL , BUT ALSO A LARGE POPULATION OF WORLD TRAVELLER-WORKERS.

A WALKING CITY

After a 1963 exhibition at the Institute of Contemporary Arts in London – *The Living City* – Archigram were supported by the influential architectural critic Reyner Banham who helped them to worldwide prominence, and their ideas were sometimes echoed by local groups abroad. One of these groups was Metabolism.

Metabolism

Although Metabolism shared some of Archigram's techno-visionary ideas about expendable buildings, they were always a more diffused group for whom architectural theory was only one strand of their activity. The group was formed in 1960 on the occasion of the Tokyo World Conference on Design. The leading architectural figure in Japan at the time was Tange Kenzo, who designed the Peace Centre, Hiroshima (1949-55) and he was the instigator of the Metabolism Group which was initially led by Kikutake Kiyonori and Kurokawa Kisho and later augmented by Maki Fumihiko and Ohtaka Masato. Their theoretical urban spaces, like Archigram's, were full of science-fiction possibilities and reflected a very 60s buoyant feeling of flux and change.

Although some buildings did emerge from individual group members, Metabolism's main concern lay in its dialectic treatment of the perceived tension between public spaces and private places – the latter often expressed as tense little space capsules, still waiting to be invented. The group's last rallying point was the Osaka World's Fair of 1970 after which its cohesion and optimism began to dwindle.

Architext

Architext was another Japanese theory-driven group, this time formed in the early 1970s by Aida Takefumi, Azuma Takamitsu, Miyawaki Mayumi, Suzuki Makoto and Takeyama Minoru.

Rather more nihilist and diverse in their opinions than their predecessors, Architext did at least share a rejection of the traditional schools, movements and doctrines in architecture. Less a group, more a non-group, Architext argued for pluralism, dislocation of tradition, individuality and confrontation.

Cedric Price b.1934

Cedric Price has been a practising architect in London since 1960, and it is no exaggeration to say that for a man who has built very little, he exerts wildly disproportionate influence among many architects all over the world who have come into contact with him and his ideas. More radical than the 60s radicals whose fire went out with the Zeitgeist, Price has continued to develop theories which refuse to deviate from the premise that architecture is not about making the reputations of architects, rather it is about responding to the genuine needs of society. The various means he proposes to achieve this are usually temporary, mobile, recyclable and adaptable – structures as responsive social tools to be used as and when necessary to improve the public's enjoyment of the urban fabric.

A typical Price scheme is his Magnet project in which a series of short-life structures are proposed to operate like urban levers, valves, platforms and conduits to generate new types of views, retreats, aspects and information access. Not only are these structures not monuments, they are hardly even structures in any recognized sense since they are usually proposed simply as drawings whose ambiguity is calculated to draw people into participating in the design process themselves.

Price's commitment to the process of urban design rather than the formal nature of its buildings is what recommends him to a whole generation of architects who have seen their own idealism pulled in every direction by working with the status quo instead of outside it.

below A bridge-like structure which transcends the landscape, part of Cedric Price's Magnet project

camera obscura

The Hudsucker Proxy

Apart from the most principled of architectural theorists, the only other professionals who can have the city the way they want it are film makers.

In their artful 1994 film *The Hudsucker Proxy* the Coen Brothers created one of the most extraordinary artificial cities in the history of movie-making. Their metropolis was a chimera based upon a 1930s New York City reproduced through models and sets and then dislocated in time for a fantastical plot set in the 1950s. The Coens, director and producer, had delayed making the film for several years until they could finally command a big enough budget to build the hybrid city of their dreams, even though they could have made the film sooner and much more cheaply using genuine period footage of old New York. However the real thing was no good to them – their city and interiors had to be purpose-built with a rich array of architectural and design references in order to be a plausible setting for the fairy tale they had in mind.

The cinema, because of its visual nature, has from the beginning been fascinated with creating fictional architecture. Science fiction writers might spend pages describing the environments of a hypothetical future, but their fantasies usually worked best when filmed. Why should this be? After all Jules Verne and H.G. Wells were not just writers of pulp fiction, and Wells in particular was a creditable novelist in other genres. It is simply because the film versions necessarily had to show not only the principal structures and gadgetry of the hypothetical world, but also its built surroundings as well; something which the writer might sketch in with general descriptions had to be realised by art and production directors in often considerable detail. The result could be 'verisimilitude' of a high degree.

The Cabinet of Dr. Caligari

When film had no original piece of writing and had to depend upon on its own effects, the power of architecture might be not only undiminished but accentuated. The German film *The Cabinet of Dr. Caligari* (1919) was made when most films were based on existing novels. In this case however Hans Janowitz and Carl Mayer wrote an original screenplay based on the real life unsolved murder case of a girl killed during a carnival. The film turned out a deeply pessimistic view of post-war Germany that used Expressionism as a result of a casual suggestion that the sets might be made from stylised painted canvasses.

Director Robert Wiene employed Expressionist designers Hermann Warm, Walter Rohrig, and Walter Reimann, who between them produced a disturbing confection of distorted perspectives, acute angles, and crazy off-vertical walls, doorways and street furniture. As an evocation of a disturbed mind it was grotesquely good and taken to such extremes that, in the end, the architecture seemed to absorb and condition the entire action, seeping into the costumes and even the weirdly constrained movement of the actors.

As designer Hermann Warm remarked '(Normally) sets should remain as background in front of which the action takes place... in Caligari this

above Even more than film makers, artists working on the pulp science fiction magazines in America from the 30s though to the 50s were able to give free rein to their imaginations to create fantastic urban metropoli

relationship is reversed. In this special case I will concede that the sets became the major means of expression'.

The original director for *The Cabinet of Dr. Caligari* was going to be Fritz Lang. Eight years later Lang – the son of an architect – was to direct one of the most famous examples of architecture-as-film-star ever made.

Metropolis

Metropolis is set in the year 2000, and concerns a vast mechanised city ruled by a tyrant capitalist and powered by a subterranean workforce of slaves. After a romantic encounter the tyrant's only son turns his back on the privileges of the city, deserting his class to join the exploited classes below. H.G. Wells thought it 'quite the silliest film', but Hitler liked it so much he tried (without success) to get Lang to direct Nazi movies.

The extraordinary power of the film's architecture is quite remarkable, which makes it all the more surprising that some of the initial concepts reflected a very different vision of Metropolis 2000. Erich Kettelhut and Otto Hunte were two of the film's principal art directors and the first version of downtown Metropolis was strangely benign in appearance. Traffic moves easily on several levels; pedestrians appear to be amiably shopping; the city's focal point is a Gothic cathedral surrounded by old houses.

Some skyscrapers in the foreground were based on many of the concepts recently devised by German architects otherwise unemployed due to the declining economic situation. In the middle distance a curved glass skyscraper, undeniably Miesian in appearance, stands at an intersection.

This drawing by Kettelhut survived although little of its recommendations did. In a brisk reminder of why he was the man in the director's chair, Fritz Lang crossed out the Gothic Church and scribbled "Away with the church; Tower of Babel instead". The eventual version of the city was to be an extraordinarily bleak, monumental and oppressive one. It was still full of hints and relics of 1920s Germany but it was also a uniquely successful entity in itself and remains a defining moment in the depiction of architecture in film.

Citizen Kane (1941) is so well known as to need little introduction or explanation. Orson Welles' use of architectural effects is as prodigious as his use of almost every others tool open to the film director. Even so it is worth recalling how the film's potent visual repository is almost exclusively one of grand spatial effects: the high wrought-iron fencing with its filigree initial 'K'; Xanadu beyond with its castle on top of a bleak man-made mountain; great shafts of light coming through high windows; the spatial tricks – the camera moves through a skylight to an interior; Kane and his increasingly estranged wife seated at either end of a long dining table.

The Fountainhead

Once much admired, at least for its intentions, *The Fountainhead* (1949) plays better today as right-wing camp comedy than as the serious tract on artistic principle it once claimed to be; however it remains a priceless film in terms of its architectural content. When the architect hero's design for a public-housing project is altered, he dynamites the building and justifies

below   Set in the year 2000 A.D., the vision of the future city as seen in Fritz Lang's 1926 epic *Metropolis*

his action with a protracted courtroom attack on collectivism. Ayn Rand's 1943 novel provided the story and the overripe dialogue. Hero Howard Roark – played by Gary Cooper at his least comfortable – was based on Frank Lloyd Wright, and the director actually tried to get Wright to design the buildings, without success.

Wright himself appeared to be flattered by Ayn Rand's attention (he designed a house for her, unbuilt, in 1946) and wrote to her saying 'Your grasp of the architectural ins and outs of a degenerate profession astonishes me'.

In the end the art director of *The Fountainhead*, Edward Carrere, seems to have been responsible for the numerous architectural models, some of which seemed to put the emphasis in the wrong place. The moral of the film is that Roark and Modernism champion the creative individual while historicism and its adherents equal the played-out force. Roarke's teacher, loosely based on Louis Sullivan, shows some unbuilt projects which actually look rather good, certainly better than Roark's pivotal housing project whose fatally flawed cantilevers were gleefully spotted by architects in the audience. Perhaps the final word on *The Fountainhead* came from the journal of the American Institute of Architects which reassessed the film on its 50th anniversary thus:

'The key to reading *The Fountainhead* today is not to see Howard Roark as a role model, but as the ultimate bad boy of American architecture'.

Blade Runner

Rather like *The Cabinet of Dr. Caligari, Blade Runner* (1982) is a film whose urban setting is so powerfully conveyed that it threatens to overwhelm everything else. The urban sprawl characteristic of the City of Angels is rendered unrecognizable, the Los Angeles of 2019 is depicted as a terminally polluted city, dark and claustrophobic and permanently wet from the only kind of rain L.A. sees on a regular basis – the artificial kind that makes the nighttime streets gleam slickly for the camera. The sets are totally bizarre and wonderful, conforming well to director Ridley Scott's instruction that he wanted to make an extraordinary film set, '40 years hence made in the style of 40 years ago'.

There are recognisable survivors from the real Los Angeles in this futuristic version – notably the Bradbury Building, one of the downtown district's unexpected delights – a five-storey inner court with French ironwork, Belgian marble, and Mexican tile.

Otherwise this is largely a composite portrait, achieved – literally – by using film montage technique. Lawrence G. Paull, the film's production designer, gave this account of how he created a very specific architecture for this grimy dystopia:

'I brought in all the photographs from Milan, and we took photographs of arcades, columns, Classical things, and all the architecture. I brought in just about my entire architectural research library, and we went from Egyptian to Deco to Streamline Moderne to Classical, from Frank Lloyd Wright to Antonio Gaudí. We turned the photographs sideways, upside down, inside out and backwards to stretch where we were going and came up with a street that looked like Conan the Barbarian in 2020'.

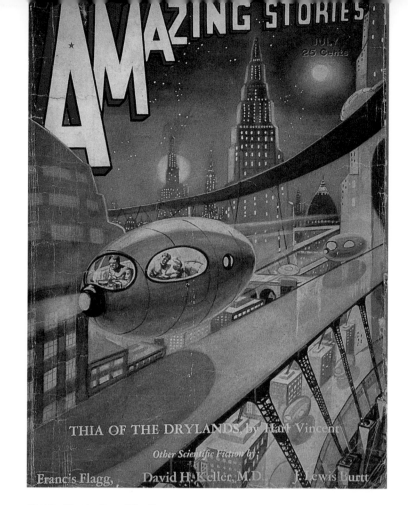

above Monorails and floating cars abounded (here we have both) in the urban transport systems envisaged by the science fiction illustrators

Miscellanea

The films mentioned here – with the possible exception of *The Fountainhead* which tends to take a rather stolidly literal approach to its subject – have all been enhanced by creating a complex and coherent architectural view of the city. These films are all palpable fictions, but without their architecture they are just as unviable as fiction as a real live city would be without its architecture. Could we even imagine such a thing? What would be left?

In recent times this tendency to give cinematic universes an appropriate and often elaborate built environment is on the increase. *Brazil* (1985), all the *Batman* films (from 1989), *Dick Tracy* (1990), *Barton Fink* (1991) and *City of Lost Children* (1995) are all films indivisible from their bespoke architectural contexts. In fact there have always been films that create their own architectural settings on a grand scale, but they are not the only ones for which fictional built environments have been created to good dramatic effect .

Certain films, less ambitious in their production values, have been equally dependent upon this or that crucial building, street or town, sometimes faked, sometimes a genuine location. Alfred Hitchcock was fond of the grand finale setpiece which, as likely as not, involved a monument or great building: London's Royal Albert Hall, Mount Rushmore, The Statue of Liberty, The Forth Railway Bridge, or whatever.

However, once a student of engineering, Hitchcock always used buildings very imaginatively in less conspicuous ways too. His incomparable *Rear Window* (1954) has its fabricated Greenwich Village apartment building, windows selectively open advent calendar-like, to provide the mainspring for the entire plot.

Likewise his *Vertigo* (1958) is shot through with haunting, almost soft-focus images of the fabric of late 50s San Francisco – its famous bridge and bay, a museum, a Spanish mission with a vertiginous tower, an apartment block, and a down at heel hotel.

A steel-and-glass futuristic Paris was evoked by Jean-Luc Godard with nothing more than selective locations for his sci-fi *Alphaville* (1965).

The same steel-and-glass Paris, equally alienating for the amiable Jacques Tati in *Playtime* (1967), was this time full of false reflections and unfathomable shifting office tower blocks.

The vast interior of the open plan Modernist office where Jack Lemmon as C.C. Baxter toils in *The Apartment* (1960), actually had its serried ranks of anonymous desks and workers artificially extended with a perspectival backdrop to underscore the effect.

Finally, and perhaps most evocatively of all, one recalls the rich environmental gumbo of *A Streetcar Named Desire* (1951). Here houses, locales and street names punctuate the present and the past. To get to her sister's run down apartment, Blanche DuBois takes one streetcar named Desire (named for a New Orleans street), then another named Cemetery, to alight in the part of the French Quarter called Elysian Fields.

The lost family house from the rapidly disappearing genteel South is called Belle Reve. Throughout the film lost youth and forgotten towns, noisy bars, screaming neighbours, a bowling alley and the cries of street

below From 1929, a fabulous airborn city with craft ferrying the inhabitants from the land below

right A more recent impression of the near future, the Gotham City of the 1992 movie *Batman Returns*

vendors punctuate and define the drama even if the audience never gets to see anything but a single room in the low-rent, two-storey apartment where the action takes place, all paper-thin walls and dangerously tropical temperatures.

In the long history of architecture in the cinema, *A Streetcar Named Desire*, in the way that it clings to the manners of its original stage productions, achieves its own brand of minimalism in a fake New Orleans. Less, for once, is more.

Postscripts

This brief investigation of theoretical and fantasy architecture was prompted by nothing more than the thought that any human activity which merits the expenditure of so much creativity, skill and passion in its abstract, fantastic or theatrical form is even more assured of continuing vigour in the real world. We have lost innumerable buildings not just through the ages but during the last century, and despite the many photographs and drawings, we can now never experience them as they were meant to be experienced.

It is therefore ironic that we can still experience Orson Welles' Xanadu, Fritz Lang's Metropolis and even the Los Angeles of *Bladerunner* – plus thousands of other celluloid cities – still functioning exactly as they were meant to. More ironic still, we also have, if we want them, the ambitions, proposals and utopian fantasies of past and present architectural theorists. Their schemes too are immutable, preserved better than the ruins of Pompeii, and available to any future archaeologist who, using digital retrieval methods rather than physical excavation tools, may find in them romance, rationalism and an unsuspected – and unintended – fresh relevance for the city of the future.

Executive Editor **Mike Evans**

Editor **Humaira Husain**

Production Controller **Julie Hadingham**

Picture Research **Claire Gouldstone**

Art Director **Keith Martin**

Senior Designer **Geoff Borin**

First published in 1998 by **Hamlyn**, an imprint of Octopus Publishing Group Limited, 2–4 Heron Quays, London E14 4JP

First published in paperback 1999

Copyright © 1998 Octopus Publishing Group Limited

A Catalogue record for this book is available from the British Library

ISBN 0 600 60004 1

Printed and bound in China

Jacket: **AKG**/H. Bock, top **Robert Harding Picture Library**/Michael Jenner, bottom **Tony Stone Images**/Simeone Huber, centre bottom **View**/Dennis Gilbert, centre top

Air Vue /Thomas d'Hoste 135 **AKG, London** 19, 25, 67, 69 top, 124, 156 left, 158 /Erik Bohr 4 bottom right, 148/149, 152 bottom /H. Bock 164 /Keith Collie 160, (copyright ARS, NY and DACS, London) /John Hios 31 top /Hilbich 66, 97, 157 /Erich Lessing 24 right, 45, 100 /Schutze/Rodeman 156 right **Fratelli Alinari** 86 **Architectural Association Picture Library** /Tom Clark 168 top /Joe Kerr 141 **Arcaid** /Alex Bartel 43 /Ian Bruce 128 left /Richard Bryant 60, 167 top, 170, 176, 177 /David Churchill 155 left © ADAGP, Paris, DACS, London 1998 /Niall Clutton 171 /Richard Glover 48 top, 48/49 centre, 152 top /Farrell Grehan 89 bottom /Peter Mauss Esto 167 bottom /Richard Waite 4 bottom left, 94/95 **Archigram Archives** /Ron Herron 182, 183 **Axiom** /Jim Holmes 47 right, 146 /James Morris 18, 28 left, 31 bottom, 32, 46 right, 87, 105, 113, 172 bottom **Bridgeman Art Library** /British Museum, London 33, /Galleria Nazionale delle Marche, Urbino 82 bottom **Caisse Nationale des Monuments Historiques et des Sites** /J. Feuillie 115 **Private Collection** 29 **Conway Library** 153 **Corbis** /Tony Arruza 139 /Richard A. Cooke 10 /Dean Conger 17 /Eye Ubiquitous 69 bottom /Kevin Fleming 140 /Chris Hellier 35 /John Heseltine 76 /Angelo Hornak 73 bottom, 98, 161 right /Wolfgang Kaehler 28 centre, 28 right /Leonard de Selva 180 /Library of Congress 119, 125 /Reverend Arthur W. V. Mace, Milepost 92 1/2 126 /Michael Nicholson 4 top left, 50/51 /Christine Osborne 59 /Richard Smith 151 /Lee Snider, Photo Images 138 /Patrick Ward 61, 62 bottom /Nik Wheeler 4 top right, 6/7, 63 left /Roger Wood 26, 57 /Adam Woolfitt 63 right, 101, 142, 169 **Corbis-Bettmann/UPI** 145 bottom, 168 bottom, Andre de Wet 166 **Cedric Price** 184 **Richard Davies** 175 **Edifice** /F.A. Duquesney 127 **The Frank Lloyd Wright Archives** /ARS, NY and DACS, London 1997 145 top left, 145 top right **Sonia Halliday Photographs** 14, 15 **Robert Harding Picture Library** 110 /Didier Barrault 89 top /Alain Evrard 20 /Nigel Francis 5 centre right, 128 right, 136/137, 147 left, 161 left /Gascoigne 116 top /K. Gillham 12 /Simon Harris 5 bottom centre left, 62 top, 114, 120/121 /F. Jalain 71 /Michael Jenner 5 top left, 22/23 /Paolo Koch 21 /Thomas Laird 5 bottom left, 162/163 /John Miller 42 /Nigel Francis 5 centre right /Roy Rainford 30, 48 bottom, 133 /Walter Rawlings 173, 190/191 /G.R. Richardson 117 /Michael Short 24 left /Adina Tovy 2/3 /H. Veiller 172 top /Adam Woolfitt 73 top /Jim Zuckerman 34 **Hirmer Verlag** 16 **Angelo Hornak** 52, 72, 103, 143 **Hulton Getty Picture Collection** 38, 40 left, 40 centre, 40 right, 80, 84 top, 90, 99 top, 104 bottom, 111, 112, 123, 130, 131, 144, 159 /Steve Eason 13 top, 13 bottom **Index** 99 bottom /Barbieri 46 /47, 54, 55, 56, 88, /Cantarelli 96 /Lensini 82 top **Interfoto** /Weltbild 102 **Caroline Jones** 4 bottom centre, 93, 106/107 **Kobal Collection** /Warner Brothers 189 /UFA 186 **Reed Consumer Books Ltd.** 5 bottom right, 178/179, 181, 185, 187, 188 **Rex Features** /Sipa Press 155 right **Agenzia Fotografica Luisa Ricciarini, Milan** /Nimatallah 83, 91 /Roberto Schezen 44 /Work in Progress 46 left /WPS 74 **Science Photo Library** /CNES, 1993 Distirbution Spot Image 8 left /Earth Satellite Corporation 9 right /Geospace 9 left /Restec, Japan 8 right **Scope** /Jean Luc Barde 5 top right, 36/37 /Jacques Guillard 41, 154 © ADAGP, Paris, DACS, London 1998 /Michel Guillard 109 /Noel Hautemaniere 68, 132 top **Tony Stone Images** 1, 5 top centre left, 78/79 /Doug Armand 132 bottom /Suzanne & Nick Geary 116 bottom /Frank Herholdt 147 right /Steven Rothfeld 84 bottom /Alan Smith 118 /Stephen Studd 4 centre top right, 39, 64/65 **View** /Denis Gilbert b & f endpapers, 174.